SCARLETT SAYS

Scarlett Moffatt was born in Bishop Auckland. She is
one of the stars of the BAFTA-winning hit Channel 4 show
Gogglebox. In 2016 she was crowned Queen of the Jungle,
winning *I'm a Celebrity Get Me Out of Here*.

Scarlett Moffatt

SCARLETT SAYS

PAN BOOKS

First published 2016 by Boxtree

First published in paperback 2017 by Pan Books
an imprint of Pan Macmillan
20 New Wharf Road, London N1 9RR
Associated companies throughout the world
www.panmacmillan.com

ISBN 978-0-7522-6602-2

3 5 7 9 8 6 4 2

A CIP catalogue record for this book is available from the British Library.

Printed and bound by CPI Group (UK) Ltd, Croydon, CR0 4YY

Visit **www.panmacmillan.com** to read more about all our books
and to buy them. You will also find features, author interviews and
news of any author events, and you can sign up for e-newsletters
so that you're always first to hear about our new releases.

For Mam, Dad and Ava Grace,

my favourite people in the whole wide world.

In memory of Grandma Frieda.

Contents

Introduction: Scarlett says . . . hello *1*

1: Scarlett says . . . meet the family *11*

2: Scarlett says . . . get glammed up *19*

3: Scarlett says . . . failing to prepare is preparing to fail *29*

4: Scarlett says . . . time to get ready *61*

5: Scarlett says . . . choose your clothes *77*

6: Scarlett says . . . cheers! *117*

7: Scarlett says . . . time to move on to the pre-drinks *177*

8: Scarlet says . . . choose a venue *205*

9: Scarlett says . . . taxi! *237*

10: Scarlett says . . . me head hurts *245*

Acknowledgements 273

Introduction

SCARLETT SAYS

. . . *hello*

A PIE CHART OF WHAT'S IN MY HEAD
8% MEMORIES I TRY AND FORGET FROM DRUNKEN NIGHTS OUT
30% INTELLIGENCE
12% THINKING ABOUT ONLINE SHOPPING
25% SARCASM
5% THINKING ABOUT WHAT I CAN EAT NEXT
20% MEMORIES FROM DRUNKEN NIGHTS OUT

Alreet. If you watch the Channel Four show *Gogglebox*, you might recognize me as the one with the big hair who watches telly with me mam and dad and always sits forward in her chair.*

If you don't watch the show, you're probably thinking, *That Alan Carr looks all right in a wig*.

My name's Scarlett Sigourney Moffatt.† I'm twenty-five and I'm from Bishop Auckland in County Durham, which is closer to Inverness than London. I don't go on red carpets. If a photographer ever shouted out, 'Who are you wearing?' I'd be like, 'Me mam's top, me mate Sarah's jeans and some shoes from the Topshop sale.'

But I do have this book, which I am very excited about. People where I'm from don't tend to write many books, so I'm

---

* Which by the way is my God-given right, because it's my front room. If I want to sit around in me pants, smearing human excrement on the walls, I can.

† I'm named after that massive whore Scarlett O'Hara from *Gone with the Wind*. Mam says that's unfair and she just tried to make the best of things in difficult circumstances. Me dad wanted to name me after Sigourney Weaver cos he loves the film *Alien*, so they played a game of Scrabble to decide and she won. I like to think I don't live up to me first name, although I did get an A* in textiles at school so I could probably make a canny dress out of some curtains.

hoping it does quite well in that little Amazon chart Books>People from Bishop Auckland>People Called Scarlett Moffatt. By the way, my surname Moffatt is not to be confused with Mo Fat, Muppet, muffett or muffin.

I'm mainly excited just to be able to talk about where I'm from cos no one ever has any idea. Round my way, there are lots of people with ponies in their garden and I had a mate come round who was like, 'It's dead posh round here, everyone has a pony.' And I had to tell her, 'Those are not posh ponies.'

And no one wears coats either. The first time I went to London, I went into a River Island and I just wandered about amazed because there was a whole 'coat section'. In the River Island near me there are two coats and nobody buys them anyway. If you wear an outdoor layer or tights, people know you're from out of town. My theory is that it's all connected to the pasties and tea. If you go down the local high street on a weekday morning, half the kids are covered in pastry crumbs. I call them the pasty kids. They're eating pasties and drinking cold tea out of their baby bottle. I reckon that's what gives so many of us superpowers that stop us from feeling the cold.

Anyway, I can't sing and I can't bake, so the only time someone like me normally gets on TV is if I'm mortal drunk, flashing my tits, or my fiancé is really crap at planning a wedding. But instead I'm on this amazing show where they film my opinions every week. I mean, not everyone thinks they're good opinions, but still. I think *Gogglebox* should get credit just for having people with accents you don't normally hear on television. I can switch on the telly most nights and there's no one like me on. That's one of the reasons people seem to like the show, because it celebrates normal people.

Loads of people on social media are dead nice and say they really enjoy what I say. And I think a lot of that's because there just aren't many programmes that listen to what young women from the north think.[*]

Then there are a few men (it's always men) who message me on Twitter to talk about the way I look – my hair, my fake tan, my weight – and I just think if they watch *Gogglebox* and that's what they take away from it, I feel sorry for them. I heard a comedian talking about people being mean on the internet once and she said you just need to imagine all the men that write this stuff sitting in their pants in their parents' basements, their fingers orange with Dorito dust, and you immediately feel better.

There's also a fair few people who assume that because I've got a fake tan, fake eyelashes and hair extensions I'm thick. I was on Twitter a little while ago and this guy just kept saying how stupid I was and how I could spell FUDGE with my exam results. I was like, '13 GCSEs, 3 A Levels, a 2:1 degree and a job as an assessor for medical evidence.' Then I just sent him two thumbs-up. What was worse was that he didn't even have a photo for his profile, he was just an egg. I felt like saying, 'Don't fucking start with me, you haven't even hatched.'

It's more of a general thing, though, isn't it? I don't know who made these earth rules, but apparently you can't be an intelligent woman and have a tan or get your hair done. Or,

---

[*] I mean, there's plenty of weirdos too. This one guy on Twitter asked me to send him a pair of me socks. Loads of people have asked me if it's me real parents I sit with or actors. What goes on in some people's heads?!

at least, if you are someone who gets your hair done, everyone assumes you can't be intelligent.*

And it's not just nutters on Twitter who are more interested in what you look like. Now I've been on telly a bit, I get rung up all the time by magazines who are like, 'Scarlett, we'd love to have you in the magazine.' And then there's always this pause. 'So have you lost any weight, or gained any weight?'

So in my book I'm not talking about weight loss, or diets, or any of that crap. And it's definitely not going to be a book that's all about lads. Have you ever heard anyone on *The Only Way is Essex* or *Made in Chelsea* talking about something that's not a drama about a lad? It's literally ridiculous. I've got a nine-year-old sister, and the idea that in the future all anyone will think about is what she looks like, what she had for lunch and who she fancies, rather than the amazing, clever, funny stuff she says, makes me feel so angry. And sad at what people would be missing out on.

But that doesn't mean I'm sitting here in a homemade wicker cardigan. I'm a huge fan of the drag queen RuPaul, and he has this great quote: 'We're born naked and the rest is drag.' Getting fake-tanned is fun, getting dressed up and doing your hair and doing your make-up is fun. And if you enjoy getting really fit and find it fun, then do it. But do it

---

* Having said that, if you look at that *University Challenge*, the opposite is definitely true. Seriously, very smart people, but most of them look like they're one step away from stealing Frodo's ring. You can recite the periodic table backwards in Latin, but you can't find the shampoo aisle in the supermarket – come on, man. I'd like to take the whole lot of them out for a drink and buy them some fake tan and a pair of shorts. 'Look: sun, fresh air, people. Go nuts.'

because you want to, not because anybody else makes you feel like you have to.

I say bollocks to bikini season, thigh gaps, thigh brows and all that rubbish. You're beach ready when you're ready to splash about in the sea like a nutter, screaming with your mates. The important thing is that you're happy with yourself, not that you look like someone who hasn't seen a biscuit for five years.*

There are people I know who think you can't be a feminist if you like clothes, which is ridiculous, but there's clearly something important not getting through.

That's one of the reasons I wanted to write a book, for any girls that watch the TV and don't see anyone like them on it. Girls that – *gasp* – want to feel like they look nice AND have people care about what they have to say. And who come from somewhere where they don't have people listening to the things they say.

The reason this book is called *Scarlett Says* is because it's my book about what me and my mates *talk* about when we're together. That's not to say we spend our time debating politics. Mainly it's stuff like whether your friends would still love you if you had no knees.† Or what if you had nipples for

---

* Anyway, rather than lose weight, you can always buy bigger jeans. Until you're wearing those 'before' photo jeans that two people can fit in. As a rule, if your clothes can fit more than one person at one time, then you should probably think about cutting down on the pies.

† You think the answer would obviously be yes, but then think how annoying it would be for them to go upstairs with you, and then when you watched TV your legs would be sticking out in front of you, and you'd be rubbish at dancing. It's a tough one.

eyes? We weren't sure if you'd also have eyes for nipples, so there was quite a lot of debate about that one. There were two camps. You'd have to have peepholes in your bra to see and some people felt that was just taking it too far.

I'm only twenty-five, so it would have been a bit ridiculous for me to write a full-on autobiography, beginning with me being born and filled with all my wisdom and stuff. I'm the first one from my family to go to university but my nine-year-old sister, Ava, is always saying stuff that makes me realize I've got no idea what's going on. She also has a bet with me that she's going to settle down before I do because it never really works out for me with the lads where I'm from. I'm just not sure how much wisdom I've really got to offer.

So I wanted to write something that tells you a bit about me but without the boring parts, something that makes you laugh and is filled with the kind of random shit I like. (I love random facts. When I tell them to my mates, they look at me like I'm a nutter. But I reckon there's always something new to learn.)

I really love a night out with me mates, so in this book I'm going to take you along on one with us while I talk about everything from Snapchat fails to shiny tights and dodgy taxi conversations – and *loads* more. So get a brew on, sit forward on your sofa and get ready to go out on the town. It'll be all of the fun, with none of the waking up in a bus shelter with doner kebab in your hair.

Top ten random facts that are definitely true

1) Bruce Forsyth is actually older than sliced bread. His mother would have had to slice her own bread until little Brucey was five months old.

2) Margaret Thatcher was part of the team that invented Mr Whippy ice cream.

3) No words in the English language rhyme with 'month', 'orange', 'silver' or 'purple' (you'll no doubt try and find some).

4) In Disney's *Aladdin*, Aladdin's face was modelled on Tom Cruise's.

5) A law that still exists to this day in England is that you cannot operate a cow whilst intoxicated.

6) More people died in 2015 from taking selfies than from shark attacks.

7) In the UK, it's illegal to eat mince pies on Christmas Day.

8) Every human being starts out as an arsehole; it's the first part of the body to form in the womb.

9) The average speed of a Heinz Ketchup squirt is .028 mph.

10) Charlie Chaplin once lost a Charlie Chaplin lookalike competition.

1

SCARLETT SAYS

...meet the family

I want to introduce you to my family first so you know who's who if you read about them in the book. They're such a massively important part of my life and I love them all to bits. I'm so lucky to have such an amazing family. My parents have been so encouraging about me doing different things and they really want me to go out and discover the world. Before *Gogglebox* I'd never been to London, but now I go all the time. Not many people go out of the DL postcode where I live, and I think me travelling about so much because of *Gogglebox* means that they've got a bit more curious too. They don't get scared when I'm going to London any more and they've also started going to new places a bit further from home.

Ava Grace, 9, sister

The poor thing, she looks so much like me we could swap heads. She is a mini version of me – seriously, she's seen photos of me when I was young and said, 'I don't remember going there?' and I'm like, 'That's because that's not you!' – but she is much funnier. She's hilarious, witty and very caring. She also knows a million random facts about life, including that strawberries are an accessory fruit and only girl wasps sting. When I go out with my sister, everyone assumes she's me daughter. They're like, 'Ooh, she looks like you.' We were at Disneyland and people took pictures of us and were going, 'Smile for your mummy,' and I told her, 'Just go with it, it'll take too long to explain.'

Because she's in year five now she has to start thinking about where she's going to go to secondary school. When she went to her first open day recently me mam put her in white socks, black shoes and black trousers. I said to her, 'You can get them off for a start.' Me mam said it was cute but she looked like Michael Jackson. Me mam also put her hair in pigtails so I took them out and straightened her hair. I know she's only young and I'm not trying to make her into something she's not, but equally I don't want her getting bullied like I did. I don't want anyone to have an excuse to say something mean to her.

Ava asks me loads of random questions all the time, about why we're here and what heaven is, and I'm like, 'Ummmm.' I just sort of make shit up. She also asks me questions about the facts of life and I never know what to say. We saw two dogs at it in the park the other day and she asked me what they were doing. I didn't want to have to go into the whole sex thing, so I said they were having a doggy hug. When we got back home she jumped on top of my mam's back and started humping it and when me mam asked her what she was doing she replied, 'I'm giving you a dog hug!' I was like, 'Nooooo!'

Elisabeth aka Betty, 45, mother

My best friend. She taught me how to speak fluent sarcasm. She has that superpower that all mothers have where you can ask them where something is in the house and they know instantly. She is very selfless, the best robot dancer I know and a top Christmas-present buyer. We have competitions to see who can write their name the neatest with their toes. I don't know why we do that, I think we get bored. Me mam always wins. It's just as if she's writing with her left hand – that's how good it looks, like. I go out drinking with her sometimes. Some of my friends find it weird but it's my mam and she's funny as. I don't get it when people get embarrassed about doing things with their family. I love it.

Mark, 50, dad

A true gentleman. He has set the standard when it comes to finding me a man because he's a legend. He's funny without knowing it and always gets things wrong. He has given me my love of conspiracy theories and aliens, and taught me never to be anything but myself. And he's the first person I'd want by my side in a zombie apocalypse.

Me dad makes me laugh because he gets words mixed up all the time. I almost encourage him to do it because it's so funny. He calls Little Mix 'Mini Mix' (I think he's getting them confused with Mini Milks, those lollies you'd have when you were a kid) and the other day we were watching *The Apprentice* and he said, 'Ooh, they've found a cliché in the market there,' instead of 'niche'.

He said to us recently that diaries can make you go to the toilet a lot. We were like, 'Eh? How does that work?' Then he went, 'Oh, no, I mean "dairy", not "diary".' How does his mind even work like that? His brain has written out a sentence with the letters wrong and he just comes out with it. I told him he needs to go to the doctor's or something and get his head looked at.

Nanny, 61

Me mam's mam. She's given me any of the wit I have today. She introduced me to Norman Wisdom, Will Hay and *Carry On* films at the age of seven. She's the top quiz maker at Christmas and she taught me how to dance to Jive Bunny. Plus she keeps chocolate in her knitting cupboard. Me mam and me nanny had both had kids by the time they were my age, so I'm basically the spinster of the family. Me nanny has a ring waiting for me as soon as I'm engaged. I'm thinking of staging an elaborate *Ocean's Eleven*-type thing, so she thinks I'm engaged and I can get my hands on it.

Pappy, 66

My granddad is the top Christmas dinner and Sunday lunch maker. He loves a good laugh and his key catchphrase is 'Never in the bloody wide world.'

Aunty Kirsty, 36

She's mam to me cousins Joshua, who's nine, and Noah, who's two. They only live five minutes away from us and I always pop round for a brew. Kirsty introduced me to make-up as a child, for which I am forever grateful. She's the top host of our monthly family tea parties. Joshua and Noah are hilarious. Joshua can read a *Harry Potter* book in a day, and Noah gets us to take him to Currys because he's obsessed with Dysons.

My friends

My friends are mint and they're so important to me. I went to primary school with my best friend Sarah and we even went to uni together. I helped her to get together with her fiancé. I would trust her with my life. When I was younger I thought friendships were all about quantity, but now I realize it's much more about quality.

My other best friends are Sam, Hannah, Billy and Kelly. There's a little group of us who do everything together. They don't care that I'm on telly and it's important that they were my friends before I was on *Gogglebox*. They watch it but it's not a big deal, and they'll phone me afterwards and say, 'You don't know what evaporated milk is? Seriously?'

They've all got really good jobs but no one takes themselves too seriously. Sam is an accountant, Sarah is an occupational therapist, Kelly is the sales manager for a bathroom store and queen of the fun night out, and Billy used to be an STI nurse and she's got some stories. Honestly, sometimes when we go into a nightclub, you can see someone recognize her and their face is priceless. She's always really good at never saying anything because of confidentiality, but you can just tell from their face when they see her. Hannah speaks three different languages and works for a hotel chain, but as soon as we're together we're like kids again.

When it was Easter last year, we were out in town and there were loads of decorations up of like eggs and bunnies and stuff, and there was one of Jesus. And Billy was really confused, saying, 'What's Jesus got to do with Easter?' She thought it was Christmas when he was born *and* died. I let her know that wasn't true but then we were talking about how unfair it was that Jesus had Christmas and his birthday on the same day, because he'd only get one set of presents. But then we thought, to be fair, he did get loads of presents from those kings and the shepherds so it all evens out.[*]

My friends and I are really supportive of each other. There's no jealousy there whatsoever and part of the reason your friends are your friends is because they make you feel good. If someone is feeling shit because a lad hasn't texted them back, that lad is instantly a knobhead, and if someone has been bitchy about someone in the group, we're there to make them feel better. Lads come and go, but if you've got good friends they're with you for life.

We stick together through everything. None of us are just into how we look and all we want to do when we go out is have fun. I can totally be myself in front of them. Even if I'm talking for ages about metal detectors they listen to me. We've got a proper girl code too. If one of us has been out with a boy, the rest of us have to stay away from him, and we *have* to like everything each other likes on social media.

Now, I think that's everyone, so we're ready to get going on our night out.

---

[*] I heard a brilliant story about Billy Connolly the other day. Apparently he was at an Easter procession once with his grandson and there was Jesus on the cross and his grandson said, 'Who's that?' and Billy Connolly said it was Jesus and his grandson said, 'What, *baby* Jesus?! Someone killed baby Jesus?!' And it definitely is confusing. There's not much about the difficult teenage years is there. Ten-year-old Jesus. Or like Jesus when he was having arguments with his parents. 'I don't want to be a carpenter. I hate you. You're not me real dad!'

2

SCARLETT SAYS

...get glammed up

Scarlett's Favourite Random Facts

Susami Bay in Japan boasts the world's deepest postbox, which is 10 metres underwater.

Artist Leonardo da Vinci invented scissors.

PSYCHO was the first film ever to show a toilet being flushed on screen.

Now having said this book's not all about diets and lads, I'm about to spend the first part of it talking about the massive efforts I put into getting ready when I go out. For some people, that might not make sense.

All I can say is that I feel a lot more confident when I've got make-up on and I'm wearing a new outfit. I feel like I put a whole new persona on. Some people might say I shouldn't have to put on a persona to feel confident and THAT'S THE WHOLE POINT, SCARLETT, but that's something I think we can leave for debating on a Monday morning, rather than a Friday night.*

The only thing I know is that when I'm getting ready to go out with my friends, it makes me really happy. I don't feel like I'm doing it for anybody else.

---

* I feel like at least one area where things are becoming more equal between the sexes is the amount of time lads spend getting ready, especially up north. It's probably the wrong way round. Women should feel like they can spend less time on their appearance, rather than blokes spending more. But I take equality where I can find it. I reckon it's the law that you have to go to the gym if you're a man up here. You go down south and some of the men are skinny and don't have sleeve tattoos. It's weird. Even so, I reckon they need a good few more years of back, sack and cracks before they get anywhere close to the shit most women put themselves through every morning just to go to work.

Everyone worries about their appearance. I reckon it's better to be honest about that, so I'm just going to get it all out the way in one go upfront.

I was a funny-looking kid. I had a big football head and a monobrow, even when I was really little. Me mam got my ears pierced when I was eight months old, maybe to make me look prettier, but I think that's child abuse. I always say to her, 'Mam, I did not need accessories at that age.' What possessed her to do that? Why would you put a needle through a baby's ears for fashion? I clearly wasn't arsed about having little gold studs back then. She says people used to think I was a boy, so maybe that's another reason she did it? So people actually knew I was a girl? Me mam used to say I was cute but I don't think I was to be honest. I think she's just saying that. She says that all the old ladies on the bus used to stop her and tell her what pretty eyes I had. I reckon that means we just got on the bus a lot. Basically we rode back and forth on the number 6 bus till someone said they liked me eyes. Then we could go home.

As I got older, I could eat an apple through a letterbox with my teeth, my massive monobrow was like Ed's from *Ed, Edd n Eddy* and I had a bright orange face because I was fake-tanned for ballroom dancing. I didn't own any straighteners so I had hair like Sideshow Bob, and the result was a very odd-looking, awkward girl.

On top of all that, my dentist wanted to give me a head brace. I'm not being funny, but the one thing that could have made me even *less* cool at that moment in time was a head brace. I got the piss taken out of me enough for the way I looked as it was, and he wanted to send me to school with a fucking head brace on? He could have saved a lot of time and cut out the middleman by locking me in a room and shouting insults at me through a megaphone himself.

I remember telling me mam a head brace was social suicide and there was no way I was going to wear one. The compromise was that I wore block braces instead, so I couldn't close my mouth and I had to walk around looking like I was constantly surprised or scared. When I look back at my massive 'brows, giant hair, weird-coloured face and permanently half-open mouth, leaving aside the fact that anyone that bullies someone is a massive dick, it's pretty obvious why I was a target for bullying.*

I also liked programmes that all my mates thought I was weird to watch. I loved *Red Dwarf*, *The Young Ones*, *Blackadder* and *Bottom*. I used to really fancy Rik Mayall in that. I cried so much when he died. Watching all that stuff is where I got my sense of humour from. I used to love *Steptoe and Son*, but when I talked about it at school everyone looked at me like I was mad, so I'd shut up about it. That and the fact I did ballroom dancing (which we'll come back to a little bit later), which everyone called old-fogie dancing, meant that I was basically socially untouchable at my school.

I used to love the Jacqueline Wilson books when I was little. And me dad said to me the other day, 'When you were a kid you always used to want us to die or for you to turn out to be adopted. You used to say, "Please can you put us in the foster home for a week, just so I can have an adventure."'

---

* The funny thing is that I still see a lot of the people who bullied me around town and these days they look like I did back then, so I reckon I was just ahead of me time.

I used to ask them to leave me in a B and B because I always thought it would be amazing to be brave under difficult circumstances. I was dead jealous of Tracy Beaker.

I also believed in Father Christmas till I was twelve. I was in year eight and I remember the teacher saying something about Santa not being real and I put my hand up and said, 'Sorry, what did you say?' And everyone really laughed so I had to pretend I was joking, but then I went home and I was devastated. 'Why did you not tell me? I looked like such a weirdo.' And me mam was just like, 'I'm really sorry, I just wanted to keep you as a kid as long as possible.'*

I was one of those kids that wore my hair in two plaits until I was far too old. Some kids at my sister Ava's school now wear make-up and that's a primary school!

It wasn't until I was fourteen, and I came back from the summer holidays before year ten, that a load of things happened at once to change things. I discovered plucking your eyebrows, the braces came off, I got some really cheap (quite shit) hair straighteners, puberty kicked in† and suddenly everyone wanted to be my friend.

All of this is just to say that I think sometimes you can be made to feel like you're weak or something if you want to fit in. Quite often you'll get some amazing, beautiful person tell-

---

* Speaking of which, I don't trust the tooth fairy, man. They come and get your teeth and leave money. So that means that human teeth are worth money to them. How long will it be before some innovative tooth fairy is like, 'Hang on, ladies, we don't need to wait for them to fall out, we can get stuck in with a hammer and have all the teeth we want.' Creepy little bastards.
† Boobs.

24

ing you that what you've got to do is be yourself. That the right thing to do is to walk your own path and all that. But the problem is, it can be really lonely on your own path. You can be yourself as much as you like, but being yourself might mean you want to fit in.

Like most girls, I have been on diets in the past but they always last about two days. As soon as you say you're on a diet all you want to eat is sugar and carbs. I did a detox diet once which was supposed to rid my body of toxins, but I got such a bad headache that after two days I went to Asda and bought myself a baguette and some Lurpak and I nearly ate the entire tub of butter. Now, I'm not saying do that as a regular thing, but I also don't reckon living on hot water, cayenne pepper and maple syrup is the way to go.

I think there's too much emphasis on what people look like. People now don't eat as much chocolate at bloody Christmas because they're worried about how they'll look on a beach six months later. It's six *months* away. Life is too short.

Now I don't even bother with dramatic health kicks. I do try and cut out crap as much as possible but I hate that feeling of guilt if you fall off the wagon when you're on a more extreme diet. It makes you feel worse than ever and half an hour later you find yourself in KFC ordering one of everything on the menu, with extra fries. The bottom line is your life is not going to get magically better if you lose a few pounds. But cake is definitely delicious. Eat the cake!*

---

* Obviously, I'm not saying be crazily unhealthy, and there are probably people who need to be careful with what they're eating. But I reckon there's such a lot of noise in the opposite direction, especially now from

My friend has a theory that it's all about making women as weak and small as they can be. If they're not eating, then they've got no energy to make noise. They're basically these shaky little pale things in the corner that don't take up any space. Any diet that doesn't give me the energy to dance for four hours with my mates isn't for me.

There's that saying 'Nothing tastes as good as skinny feels'. Whoever came up with that, you haven't eaten enough types of food, man. I could list you five things right this minute, just beginning with the letter M, that taste more delicious.

These days I really don't mind if people like me or not. I would never change who I am to fit in with how other people may want me to be. But I totally get that desire to be like everyone else and the feeling you get when you think you never will be. I've never forgotten what it's like to feel on the outside of everything and that's why my friends are so important to me, because they're people I can have a laugh with, rather than people who just stand around the edge of the dance floor looking cool. When being nice and kind gets you nowhere, don't change the person you are, change the people you're talking to!

---

this new lot of big-hair yoga women who spiralize everything. If someone offered me some courgetti, they'd be wearing it.

Know your north-east slang!

Geordies: those from Newcastle. Or, as we say, the Toon. Not to be confused with . . .

Mackems: Sunderland folk

Smoggies: those from Middlesbrough, home of the parmo (deep-fried chicken in breadcrumbs topped with béchamel sauce and cheese)

County Durhamers: the greatest of the north-easterners. Also known as Durhamites and pit-yakkas. Durham is the birthplace of Denise Welsh, Mr Bean and, of course, the Moffatts

Way, aye: yes, or of course

Howay, man: come on or hurry up

Gan yam: going home

Marra: friend

Mortal: drunk

Scran/bait: food

Bairn: child

Radgie: a really crazy person or when you are in a mood

Gadgie: anyone who has male bits, basically

Canny: nice/pleasant, or a value of measure, e.g. 'That dog's canny small, like.'

Geet walla: very, very large

Netty: toilet

3
SCARLETT SAYS

...failing to prepare is preparing to fail

Scarlett's Favourite Random Facts

The GUINNESS WORLD RECORDS book is the book that gets stolen most often from public libraries.

Most Muppets are left-handed.

There are more stars in space than there are grains of sand on all the beaches in the world.

I don't know about you, but any night out with my mates will usually start with pretty much an entire week's worth of chat on our Facebook group so we can work out where we're going and what we're wearing. As soon as one weekend is over, the planning starts for the next one. There are about fourteen of us in our group but there are a couple that are just observers and don't contribute. I think it's nice that there's a real mix of people, and none of us have got any airs and graces. All of my mates are dead down to earth. I used to go out in Newcastle sometimes with another group of girls and it just wasn't the same. They were nice enough but they were really posey and not a lot of fun. They sat in booths being really sedate, sipping overpriced cocktails and not speaking to each other.

Sam or Kelly usually decide where we go. They're the shepherds and we're their sheep. We'll spend all week planning our outfits and we'll post photos of potential ones so everyone can give us feedback. It's so sad, but it's essential! I reckon a lot of the time planning a night out is more fun than the night itself.

I'll be out at work and then when I get home and check me phone at the end of the day I'll have about 176 messages to read from the group alone. I dread to think how much time everyone wastes messaging rather than doing their work.

Basically all our employers should get together and invoice Facebook for the time we all spend making the site more valuable by spending all our time on it. I can't be arsed to read all the messages so I'll ask someone for a summary at the end of the day and just get the highlights so I know what's going on.

Failbook

I don't know how humans coped before they had WhatsApp or Facebook to plan a night out. I can't get my head round the idea that they just agreed a time and a place and that was it. My dad was talking about this the other day, how when he was young you didn't have mobile phones, so you just had to make arrangements and then turn up. It blows your mind.

Facebook is definitely a great way to organize a night out but I think it becomes quite dangerous when it's the first thing you look at when you wake up in the morning. I deleted the app from me phone because I spend so much time looking at it. It's a bit of a ball-ache having to put in your email and password when you want to go on it, so my laziness means I look at it less.

The only thing I don't like about Facebook is the way people check in constantly. The worst thing is when people check in at the gym and put 'leg day' or 'abs day'. So fucking what?

I know this lad who is always sitting around messing about on his phone when I go to the gym. When I went the other day he was doing it for about an hour and when he left I saw that he'd posted, 'Hardcore workout. I'm going to have jelly legs in the morning.' What? From fucking texting?

Even when we're doing our pre-pre-drinking at one of the girls' houses me friend Sam will check us in. *Why?* Why do people need to know whose house we're at? I don't want strangers knowing my every move.

Sam even checks herself in when she's in bed. Again, *why?* The worst is when she checks us in at Bargain Booze when we're getting our drinks for the night. I don't want anyone to know I go there. She also checks us in wherever we're out eating, so if I've told me friends I'm on a health kick and then she checks us in at McDonald's, I'm done for.

I'm one of those people who is guilty of blocking people on Facebook if I fall out with them. I do it to me mam all the time. If we've had an argument, I'll unfriend her because I know she checks my Facebook a lot. It's so pathetic but if you're angry you get a little bit of pleasure out of unfriending someone. If anyone did it to me, I'd properly kick off, though.

I was really angry when I heard about the dislike button coming in. It's such an easy way to bully people. I see loads of statuses I think are twatty but I just ignore them. I think it would be mean to 'dislike' what someone writes and I hope it never happens. Sometimes when I look on Twitter it seems like some people are only there to give people grief. I genuinely feel bad for them. Sometimes I'll tweet the people who've written the nasty comments and say, 'Are you happy with your life?' I feel sad that they think it's OK to do that, and I don't get it. It's like going up to someone in the street and saying, 'Your hair's shite.' You don't know that person, so why would you say that?*

The other thing with Facebook is that it's a bit of a fantasy world for some people. They make out their lives are amazing. I know this girl who really doesn't like her boyfriend and yet she messages him where everyone can see, saying, 'Can't wait to see you later.' She could use that energy she wastes typing on dumping him.

#Datenights

Fucking #datenight. It drives me mad when people put that on social media. I just don't understand why everyone needs to know you're going out with your other half. When I've had boyfriends, I haven't felt like I have to put our every move on Facebook.

People will buy a meal and eat it at home and put up a photo saying #datenight. It's not a bloody date night; you've just bought a ready meal and you're sat in your own house with the person you live with.

---

* My theory is that the whole world is just pissed off because they used to be able to vent by slamming the phone down at the end of an argument. It was the way they got rid of all that stored-up aggression. Pushing the little button on the screen of your phone doesn't vent any of your anger, does it? They should make a cover for your phone and an app to go with it, so you can smash your smartphone onto the table and it hangs up. In fact, if that isn't already a thing, nobody steal it, that's my idea. I'm taking it to the Dragons.

Too many photos!

OK, my final moan about Facebook is this: we don't need to see pictures of *everything* people's kids do. 'Here's little Johnny eating.' 'Here's little Johnny in the car.' 'Here's little Johnny on his potty.' Unless your kid is tightrope walking or speed skating, I don't want to see that shit. I don't care if your baby is smiling. It's probably wind anyway.

And if I see one more 'first day at school' photo . . . How many kids do I need to see in their uniform? Surely parents realize that everyone else is doing it and it's *boring*? Do they think their kid is cuter than everyone else's? Me mam tried to put a photo of me little sister Ava up, but Ava refused to let her do it and she's only nine. I felt dead, dead proud of her. A friend of mine is a postwoman and she posted a photo of herself in her uniform and wrote, 'First day at big work,' which was really funny.

Actually, I lied . . .

I have one more Facebook-related thing to moan about – passive-aggressive statuses when people slag off someone else but don't name them. Or when someone posts something really cryptic like, 'So pissed off. Why do good things always happen to bad people?' People start posting, 'What's wrong, hon? You OK? Inbox me,' underneath. It's all to get attention. If you're not going to tell us what's wrong with you, don't bother to write anything. It's as bad as when people just write, 'Today is a good day.' For Christ's sake, no one is that interested in your life. You don't need to do a teaser trailer.

Back in the day

It sounds like I hate everything about it but when Facebook first started I loved it. Now anything I want to say I put on Twitter because I much prefer it. For some reason people have set up Facebook accounts in my name, so it looks like I'm on there all the time talking crap.

I mainly use Facebook for talking to me mates now, and I still like looking at other people's statuses so I know what's going on. I think it actually looks like Twitter now and I like that better because it helps me to know where I'm at with all my apps.

Way back in the day, when social media apps started popping up, I had Bebo, and if I remember rightly that was where I met my first ever boyfriend. He was at university and I was at school and I remember him driving me to get my GCSE results and feeling dead cool because he had a car. Back then that was pretty much my only requirement when it came to lads.

Bitching

I'm not naïve and I know that people gossip about me a lot more now I'm on TV. I've seen all sorts of things written about me on Facebook. One girl posted a while back, 'Scarlett thinks she's the bee's knees. She walks around with a bodyguard now.' I think she must have seen me with my friend Ivo and thought I'd bloody hired him, because he's quite a big lad. Hilarious.

Someone else put a post up saying that I think I'm too

good to go out in my own town, but I'm out in it every week! A lot of people also bring up random things I did at school over ten years ago like it's relevant. It's dead strange.

It makes me sad that it's people from my home town who are the ones that have a go at me. I love where I live but I do find that the further away from it I go the nicer people are to me. I don't know if it's because people compare themselves and wonder why they're not on TV, or what. I can't think of any other reason. It's not like I think I'm better than anyone or act any differently. I'm on a TV show once a week; I haven't morphed into fucking J-Lo. My friends would be the first people to tell me if they thought I'd changed, and I'd be mortified if I did.

Checking in

Sam is *really* good at getting gossip on Facebook. You can always tell when two people start dating because they like every single one of each other's statuses, no matter how shit they are, and she always spots it. She'll say, 'You know James? He's supposed to be with Lucy but he's liked all of Kate's photos on Facebook.' Then a week later we'll hear that James and Lucy have split up.

She noticed a while back that this guy we know, who has a girlfriend, checked in at a park on Facebook. Ten minutes later this girl we know checked in there too. It's not like it's just around the corner and they know each other so there's no way it was a coincidence. We chatted about that for over an hour trying to analyse what was going on.

It's like when people put something on Snapchat and you

can see someone in the background who really shouldn't be there. Why don't people think? We've busted a few people that way too. Sam is really good at sniffing out a story. She'd be a great secret agent or journalist.

I like a bit of celebrity gossip, and I love being the one who tells my friends when something really dramatic happens, like when a big power-couple split up. It's cool being the one to break the news and seeing my mates' reactions. We have a bit of a competition to see who can be first in with something really good.

While we are never horrible and try to get on with everyone, I will hold my hands up and say that sometimes my friends and I can get a little bit bitchy when it comes to talking about what people wear. Well, one girl in particular. She lives in my town and she wears these really thick, glossy skin-coloured tights whatever the weather. Her legs look like they're made of plastic. She used to go out with one of my friends' husbands and I think that's why we're a bit mean about her. If one of us sees her, we'll post in our Facebook group, 'Just seen shiny tights, she was buying bread in Asda.'

I shit you not, I saw her recently with mascara in her hair. It's 2015. Where can you even buy hair mascara from these days? Maybe eBay? I wouldn't be unkind if she was a nice person, but she's not, so I'm allowed.

Ten things you should never do on social media

1) Write mundane tweets or statuses
No one gives a flying monkeys if you've just changed your 4.5 tog duvet for a 13.5 tog #readyforwinter. That isn't what this shit was created for.

2) Use it as some form of Google search engine
If you have time to write a status asking what time Tesco closes on a Sunday, you have time to type that into Google and do your bloody research yourself. Unless you're trying to impress everyone by letting them know you're going to Tesco?

3) Brag
We do not need to see everything you've bought or photos of your supermarket shopping. No one cares. No one. Unless they're a food fetishist, in which case you should be on a very different website.

4) Join in an argument
I'm not going to say don't start an argument, because reading people's arguments is hilarious, but never involve yourself in someone else's unless you know exactly what's going on. Nine times out of ten you'll end up being the bad guy and have to take yourself off social media temporarily because so many people are calling you a twat.

5) Weather statuses
#itsraining. Shit, really, Miss Marple? Thank God you told me because I can't look out of a window myself.

6) Stalk an ex

Exes should be out of sight, out of mind. You're only prolonging the pain and there will come a moment when you see him with someone else and have to drown your sorrows in sambuca.

7) Catfish

Stop trying to be something you're not! It's all very well trying to create the illusion of being a millionaire playboy/girl, but you served me in Asda last week.

8) Check in everywhere you go

Checking in at work/Starbucks/Wetherspoons/the loo in McDonald's = zzzzzzz.

9) Troll

You wouldn't go up to a stranger in the street and start slagging them off and shouting, 'Hashtag slag!' at the top of your lungs, so don't do it while you're hiding behind your laptop.

10) Go hashtag crazy

I know people who hashtag twenty things when they post a photo of themselves. There's no need to take a photo of yourself and be like #photo #me #face #nose #hashtag. We get it.

Twitter

I feel like there should be some kind of helpline for Twitter addicts because my obsession is getting out of control. Sometimes I even hashtag while I'm speaking – like, 'Hashtag *awkward'* – and that is *not* OK.

Twitter is mint. You just sort of start having a conversation with yourself and hope someone joins in. If someone said to me I could only have one social app, I would choose Twitter. You find out everything that's happening because whatever is trending comes up really quickly. Sometimes you find out something is happening before it's even in the papers or on the news. It's also really good for spreading awareness of things. And it's a bloody good laugh.

I love it when people have Twitter fails and I liked the debate about whether or not that dress was blue or white that time. It didn't really matter; it was a bloody horrible dress whatever colour it was.

I've got quite a lot of followers now, which is dead flattering, but it does make me think twice about posting certain things. I don't think there's been anything I've *really* regretted because I do hold myself back sometimes, but I nearly posted something about being in a shitty mood the other day and I thought people would just think I was really moany. I do love ranting, though. I always rant during *Celebrity Big Brother.* That show gives me a lot to rant about. They go in saying they just want to really enjoy the experience and by like day three they're crying and wiping their own faeces all over the place.

People keep tweeting me at the moment to tell me I look like Jesy out of Little Mix. I reckon that's because we both wear eye make-up and have dark hair. That's it. I mean, I can see it a little bit but people are like, 'Ooh, youse could swap heads.'

Tweeting under the influence

Drunk tweets are the *worst.* I was out the other night and I tweeted, 'Why do you only know you're drunk when you're in the toilet?' It's so true. I was in a cubicle for about five minutes chatting to myself. Up until that point I'd thought I was quite sober.

I thought I'd tweeted something really deep after I drank a shitload of wine once, but when I woke up the following morning it was just a load of letters and it made no sense whatsoever.

Tweeting celebrities

Where else can you talk to celebrities you would never usually get to interact with? I chat to Amanda Holden and Eammon Holmes sometimes, and when Jonathan Ross started following me I was like, he actually knows who I am!

Some of my favourite people to follow are Alan Carr because he's so funny, and Ricky Gervais because he rants constantly. Eammon Holmes is funny and doesn't give a shit, and if someone is trending, I'll look at their tweets and maybe start following them. I also like TheLadBible and fact-based tweeters who post random stuff.[*]

---

[*] One thing I don't understand, when that Russian plane blew up and ISIS took credit for it on Twitter, is how ISIS can be on Twitter. Surely if they've got a blue tick that means Twitter is doing better than the FBI at working out who they are. It makes me sad when you fall down that wormhole and you see all of the hatred and anger people are typing to each other on Twitter. There's all those cases of people tweeting threatening stuff and you just want to say, 'Have a word with yourself, man'.

When I tweet I just stick to what I'm up to and what's on TV, mainly. But there's one topic I always feel like I have to pipe up about because there's so much shit being written constantly.

People need to stop going on about the immigration crisis. It dominates headlines and it makes people hate people for no reason. I said to me dad, 'People don't risk their lives in tiny boats and hang on to the bottom of trucks because they've heard they'll get £36.80 a week.' People will only get in a boat if they think it's safer than the land. What does that say? They're willing to risk their lives in a shitty boat because it's too dangerous to stay where they are. There are all these stories in the news all the time, and the language they use, it's like they're animals or insects, not people.

I hope a crisis like that never happens in England because at the moment it feels like everyone thinks it's not their problem. It's the lottery of life. We're only in this country because we were lucky enough to be born here, and we've got no more right to be safe than anyone else. We didn't do anything to be born here, we didn't earn it. The migrants have got families and they're just trying to do what's best for them. If you can't understand that, I don't know what's wrong with you.

Even if 200,000 people came to the UK to seek asylum, it's not going to ruin the country. We have space. The press make out that immigrants are coming over here and taking our money and food but that's ridiculous. When I see an immigrant with a £1 million bonus fucking up the financial system I'll start getting angry but until then people need to be more humane. It makes me sad that people don't care.

In fact, there we go, that's my idea. We can force all the

bankers to sponsor a family of immigrants fleeing the destruction of their homes as part of their bonus. It can be a rich twat tax, which will show up on their payslip with 'the one good thing you've contributed to society' written alongside it.

I think it's bad when people have so much money they don't know what to do with it. They lose all sense and buy things like gold toilet seats or jewel-encrusted doorknobs. Why? I was on holiday a while back and I saw a man buy a six-litre bottle of Grey Goose between him and his mate, which was about £3,000. I'm sure he was doing it just to impress people. That's compensating for something, that is.

I don't understand how nurses, who help to save lives, get paid so little, but someone who sits behind a desk watching numbers go up and down and contributes very little to society gets to be a multi-millionaire. And the thing is, they still want more. They need it to fill their empty souls. They're greedy and they're dickheads. End of.

The meaning of life

I get loads of tweets from people asking why we're here. Like, on earth and shit. I don't know why people think I'm some sort of philosopher. I sometimes reply and tell them we're in a kind of *Sims* game and we're being controlled. When we die we move on to the next level of the game.

Death

While I'm on the subject of dying, I'm not that religious or nowt but just out of sheer terror I can't really believe that when you die that's it. I feel like there must be somewhere you go. But I was saying that to Ava and she just said, 'When you're dead, that's it, you go in the ground and you get eaten by maggots. That's why it's important to live your life now and make sure it's a good one.' And, like I've said, she's nine. Honestly, they could parachute that girl in to sort out the Middle East.

Getting older

Thinking about death always makes me think about getting older. Not that at twenty-five I feel like I'm about to croak! But now that I *am* getting older, sometimes when I wake up on a Monday I still feel a little bit crap. I can definitely tell I'm not sixteen any more. When I was younger I used to put an age on everything. At twenty-three I was going to meet the love of my life, and at twenty-six I'd get married. But then you realize that life isn't like that and you have to take it as it comes. Anyway, if I held to that schedule, it'd mean I'd basically have to really crunch the gap between meeting someone and getting married. As it stands, I'd have like four months or something. That's not the way good decisions are made.

I like being a bit older now, though. You do get more responsible and take things slightly more seriously because you have to, and I can't *wait* to be properly old. I'm going to push my way to the front of queues and pretend I don't know any better, and eyeball people until they get up and offer me seats on public transport.

I'm going to be a really grumpy, fat old person. I'm going to get to a certain age and just keep eating and eating. I'm going to stop giving a shit about things. I'm going to bore the arse off my grandchildren about the good old days when you only had one dishwasher in your house and iPads weren't made of thoughts.

I feel old sometimes now when I try to explain dial-up internet to my little sister, and it's only a matter of time before I start saying, 'You don't know you're born.' She doesn't understand what videos are, and she thinks it's crazy that we used to have to go to a shop and rent a video if we wanted to watch a film.

I can tell I'm not sixteen any more because sometimes I get excited when plans get cancelled so I can stay in in my onesie. I've also started to buy a lot of candles and I've got tons of scatter cushions in my bedroom. I spend my money on interior design rather than wine and pizza. Well, sometimes anyway.

My grandma Frieda is eighty-five now and she does whatever makes her happy, and literally decides when she does and doesn't want to talk to us. She does this thing now where, if she can't be arsed to talk to you, she closes her eyes and ignores you. I walk out thinking she's asleep and when I come back in her eyes are wide open and she's watching the telly. I think it's brilliant.

I'm not going to care what anyone thinks of me when I'm properly old. I'm going to be really honest with people. Imagine how cool it will be when you can tell someone their hair looks shit and people will make excuses for you? 'Oh, she's just old. She doesn't mean it.' I bloody will. I'll have all my senses about me but I'll get away with it. Even if I can still walk to the shop I'm going to get a mobility scooter and drive there. I'm going to wear American tan tights and moan constantly. I've got a lot to look forward to.

Ten ways I know I'm becoming my mother

1) I've started buying lots of candles and scatter cushions (and getting excited about them).

2) I've started checking the weather before I go out (and taking a safety Pac-a-Mac with me).

3) I look forward to going to bed. Ooh, is it 9 p.m. yet?

4) I've started reading the *Radio Times* to check what's going to happen in *EastEnders* even though I'll be watching it that night.

5) I get excited when people cancel plans for a night out. Sometimes I just want to stay in and watch *The X Factor* with a takeaway.

6) I've started saying things like, 'In my day you could buy a chocolate bar, a packet of crisps and a drink and get change out of 50p,' or, 'Remember when penny sweets still cost a penny.'

7) When I watch a film I tend to agree with what the parents in it think/say rather than the kids.

8) I've found myself choosing sensible, comfortable shoes over fashionable ones.

9) I've actually started wearing my mother's clothes.

10) I've begun mumbling to myself about how much I've got to do in the day. 'Argh, I've got a load of washing to put on and I've got to empty the dishwasher.'

Working 9 till 5

If we're going out on a Friday night, most of the Facebook messages come through while I'm at work as it's easier for a lot of my mates to go online when they're at their jobs. But I prefer to switch my phone off and just concentrate on work while I'm there, so I have to catch up on everything at the end of the day. Most people assume I haven't got a job when they message me on Twitter. I've had all sorts of jobs. I even worked with me mam once. If you've never done it before, I can tell you it's exactly as good as you imagine it would be. I've been in my current job for a year, which is the longest I've worked anywhere. I used to last about four weeks on average before that.

When I was really young I wanted to be a bus driver. I was obsessed with the idea until I went to secondary school, when I decided I wanted to be a geography or dance teacher. I think it's scary that you have to try and decide what you want to do when you're so young and your GCSE and A Level choices can kind of determine what you go on to do. Who really knows what they want to be at that age? I used to want to be a teacher and I studied it at university. I didn't know what kind of teaching I wanted to do, and in my first year I did dance, but then I realized I didn't want to teach kids to waft around like trees. In the second and third years I did physical education, then in my fourth year I did placements in schools. That was when I realized I didn't really like kids.

My first ever part-time job was working in a newsagent's sorting out the pick'n'mix. I got paid £3.50 an hour and had access to all the sweets I could eat. Not that they knew about the last bit. Except they do now, I suppose. (If you're reading this, Mr and Mrs Simpson, I'm sorry, but £3.50 an hour?!)

My next job was on the checkouts in Asda and that was quite funny because you got some strange characters coming by. This lady used to come in at 2 p.m. every Saturday and she'd always come to my till. I think she must have been a bit OCD because she lined up all her food alphabetically on the conveyor belt. She'd start with bread and then go on to cat food, and she'd always finish with six Wispas. When I scanned them she'd shout, 'Can I have a Wispa, Wispa, Wispa . . .' loads of times. She'd gradually lower the volume until she was *actually* whispering it. I laugh at anything anyway so it was so hard trying to keep a straight face. That was a fucking challenge.

I had to ID people for all sorts and they used to get really pissed off with me. It wasn't my bloody choice. A woman once threw a packet of paracetamol at my head because I told her she could only buy two boxes at a time.

I worked on the make-up counter of a department store for a while, but I got sacked for making people too orange. When women came in to get their make-up done I always thought it was best to go a couple of shades darker, but the make-up artists weren't that keen because they're all about being *au naturel*.

The area manager came in to check on everyone's work one day and I'd already had a couple of disciplinaries for putting too much make-up on people. I did one woman's make-up as a test run for her wedding and she loved it but the area manager went crazy and said her body didn't match her face. It was pretty hard to come back from that so they gave me the boot.

I also worked at a couple of clothes shops, mainly for the discounts, but I left because the managers kept making me clean the loos.

I was a shot girl in a club for a while selling tequila but it wasn't me at all. I had to walk around in a leotard flirting with lads. I used to say, 'Are you not going to buy me a shot?' and then I'd pretend to down it and keep the money. I got so many tips there it was ridiculous.

When I was twenty, I worked as a beauty therapist for six months. I'm literally a beauty school dropout. It turns out it's really hard to wash other people's hair. I started and I was like, well, I've been washing my own hair since I was seven, so I should be pretty good at this. It turns out it's really difficult to wash someone else's hair. And then you have to do the head massage. I love getting my hair cut because I get the head massage. I reckon the world separates into people that shut their eyes at the hairdresser's when they're getting the massage and people that keep them open. I've got a friend who worries that if they shut their eyes they'll look really weird, like they're too into it, but I reckon it's even weirder to just stare at the stylist while they're doing it. It's like people who kiss with their eyes properly open, it's not right.

I even once worked in a call centre and I could never do it again because I haven't got the patience for it. I got shouted at and got death threats and all sorts. The public are crazy.

There are loads of call centres in the north-east because

I think we've got quite friendly accents, and I know at least five people who work in them.

I realize that means I should be more sympathetic but it does drive me up the wall when I get calls about PPI claims. I don't even know what PPI is? Whenever me dad gets a call he knows is a sales call he answers it by saying, 'Whitley Bay lighthouse. How can I help you?' to try and put them off.

I also don't understand why people call and ask you if you need new windows. I feel like saying, 'If I needed new windows, I would have gone and got them, mate, I wouldn't have waited until you called me.' Who are these people sat at home freezing cold with no windows but a working phone and when it rings they're like, 'Thank goodness you called, I had no idea how to fix this situation'?

Current job

If there was ever any danger of getting carried away with being on the TV, my current job always brings me right back down to earth. I work as a disability advisor helping students at university. I access the medical evidence and we work out what help and equipment they need, and try to make them feel like they're on a level playing field with everyone who is able-bodied. I didn't realize all the different conditions people can have and how they affect people until I worked there.

I've been doing it for just over a year now and it's really rewarding. It's hard work sometimes because the medical evidence can go really deep and it can be difficult when you know people are having such a hard time. You can live in a little TV bubble sometimes so it's nice to be able to do something that really makes a difference.*

The Office

My job is like being in *The Office* at times. It's hilarious. My friend Charlotte is always buying Flash wipes and cleaning everyone's desks, and she cleans everyone's keyboards once a week. It's shocking what comes out. Some people are hiding a full meal in theirs. In fact, the longer I've worked in an office, the more I appreciate the Ricky Gervais show. I'm more like Tim, though. Someone says something and I'm making a face, or making a joke and the person doesn't realize. Me mam watched *The Office* and loved it straight away. But me nanny thought it was real. I can remember her saying, 'That main boss man is a dickhead, isn't he?' No, Nanny, it's not real, it's not a documentary. And everyone doing that David Brent dance with the hands. Everyone's had a boss like that and now that I'm older I can appreciate how accurate it is. There's always a bit of a dickhead who wants to be loved and laughed at.

We have a quiz during the team meeting every Wednesday so we can do a bit of bonding and they're such nice people. I've learnt loads since I've been there. I was asking the others whether the sperm or the egg makes a baby and we

---

* Literally the week that I sent this book off to be edited, I got a job hosting a radio breakfast show up near me. It's only temporary and I've done one day, so all I can say is that it's mental getting up when there are still owls out.

had a really long conversation about it and it was really enlightening. I'm still not sure of the right answer but it was a great chat, like.

We have some very funny work nights out. I always thought a couple of my team were quite quiet, and then suddenly one evening they were lining up the Jägerbombs and doing the worm and all sorts. You can really get to know people on a night out.

All of us in the office like our food and sometimes we have buffet days where we each bring in a different dish. We had an around-the-world buffet recently when we had to pick a country out of a hat and then bring in food from that country. And we have Friday pie day where we go to Taylors nearby and order loads of pies. We have baking days as well. I don't know how we get any work done around all the eating.

There's none of that rubbish that some women do when you're like, 'Do you want to get some lunch?' and they're like, 'Nah, I'm OK, I had half an orange yesterday.' I can't be doing with that nonsense.

Gogglebox

I guess my other job now is being on *Gogglebox*.

I got involved with *Gogglebox* because I used to go to college with one of the researchers. He phoned me and said they were looking for families in the north and asked if I knew anyone who would be good for it. That was just before the third series and me mam and I were already watching it so knew it was a good show. I asked some of my friends but they weren't keen so my mate asked me if my family would try out for it, and we thought, *Why not?*

A producer came to do some trial filming and they held up some cards with various people on for us to talk about. I thought Nelson Mandela was Uncle Ben the rice man, so I was chatting away about how nice his savoury rice was. Then they showed us a picture of a really young David Cameron and I thought he was Piers Morgan, so I went off on one about him.

They said they'd be in touch, although I wasn't expecting good news after my performance, but they called a few weeks later and asked us if we wanted to join the show. When we first filmed it did feel weird having cameras in our living room but now I genuinely don't even notice them. We all feel really settled-in now and it's all very natural.

Before we joined, the show was already very popular. When it first aired it was on a Wednesday at 10 p.m. Before me and my mam and dad joined, because it had so many viewers, Channel 4 had decided to move it to 9 p.m. on a Friday, and now everyone in the country watches it!

I get a lot of people coming up to me and saying they should be on *Gogglebox* and I always tell them it's harder than it looks. When we're filming obviously we make more of a conscious effort to talk about things and be animated. We don't say anything we wouldn't usually say but you do have to put in a bit of effort, like!

I get told off by some people who watch the show because they think I swear too much and I shouldn't do it in front of me mam and dad, but I think people forget I'm twenty-five.

What I love about the show is how easily people can relate

to it. People often say to me, 'My granddad's just like Leon,' or, 'Your mam reminds me of my mam.' It's nice that people have an affinity with us and feel like they're a part of it in a way.

It's definitely the best job I've ever had.

Five jobs I would hate to do

Chef
If I was a chef, the special of the day would either be crackers with beans and cheese, tinned soup or frozen pizza, because that's where my cooking skills begin and end.

Tour guide
My family and friends always take the mickey out of the fact I'm crap with directions. I can visit a place a hundred times and I still won't know how to get there. I once rang my friend Sarah because I got lost on my way home from work because I'd left work by a different door. I ended up getting a taxi home. It was a five-minute walk.

Builder
Even as a child my Lego constructions didn't cut the mustard. I once tried to assemble a flat-pack set of drawers and ended up putting them together upside down and back to front.

Librarian

I genuinely don't think I could be quiet or whisper for that amount of time. My friends always shout at me because my whisper is just a slightly quieter version of my normal, everyday voice.

Traffic warden

For two reasons: I couldn't put up with all the hate and I'm a sucker for a sob story. I wouldn't give out any tickets so I'd lose my job.

Five jobs I would love to do

Chocolate taster

Someone somewhere actually gets paid for trying chocolate from around the world and rating it. God must have loved them.

Professional wine taster

See above. Again, what an amazing job, and one I think I'd be really good at. 'This cheeky little red would go perfectly with a doner kebab.'

Ant and Dec's sidekick

Just to spice things up a bit, the Geordie duo could become a trio. Imagine hanging out with those boys all day and having a laugh. I'd love it.

Stephen Hawking's assistant

Every day would be like a school day. All of the amazing things that used to confuse you would suddenly make sense because Stephen would explain everything to you. I love that dude.

Radio presenter

Chat shit all day. Finish work by lunchtime. It'd be mint.*

---

* I wrote this before I actually had to do it. Owls, man. Owls.

4

SCARLETT SAYS

. . . time to get ready

Scarlett's Favourite Random Facts

'Rhythm' is the longest English word that doesn't contain a vowel.

Humans can live without food for about a month, but would only last for a week without water.

Most lipstick contains fish scales.

So we've checked all the messages, we know where we're going and when. Now comes the really fun bit. I should warn you that it takes me AGES to get ready.

When I'm home from work, I can waste hours when I should be getting ready to go out. I'm always late and it drives my friends mad. Sometimes I'll just be in the bath watching YouTube videos for hours. I'll have to top up the bath like four times to keep it hot.*

YouTube

I can spend hours watching top-ten compilations about things like coincidences or conspiracy theories. I love anything titled 'Things you'll never believe are true'.

There are few things I enjoy more than a good conspiracy theory, and YouTube allows me to watch shit I would never have known about before. I love anything from space conspiracies to the ones that claim famous dead people aren't really dead. I like to think the glamorous blonde lady behind

---

* Does anyone else do that thing where they kind of scoop the hot bathwater with their hands and try and mix it around them so it warms up quicker? I'm pretty sure the science of liquids doesn't support that but I still do it every time.

the bar at my local Wetherpoons is actually Marilyn Monroe after some really extensive surgery.

Moon Landing

I really don't know if I believe that America actually put people on the moon. I think it's just something America wanted to do before the UK did and that one day it will come out that it's total crap and it was filmed in a warehouse somewhere, or on a film set in LA. I don't understand why they don't just do it again to prove that they can. You could sell advertising around the edge of the moon and make a fortune to pay for it. Everyone in the world would watch it. They could charge pay per view. If they can get all that money a year for the football, surely going to the moon would get more than that. They could do it like a reality thing too, pick one person who's not an astronaut to go along with them, and you'd get people ringing in and voting who they wanted, so they'd make money that way as well. What I'm saying is, it must be possible to do it again now, so that people believe it.

I'm also really into time-travel conspiracy theories, where people claim they've gone back or forward in time. Seriously, if they had genuinely travelled to the future, wouldn't they bring some really good shit back with them as proof? Like an iPhone that has a decent battery life? Although my experience is that battery life is getting worse, so maybe in the future it'd be even more crap.

My big theory is that when controversial stuff happens, like when Miley Cyrus did her foam hand pointing thing when she was bent over, or when Britney shaved her head, it's when there's stuff going down in the US and they need to distract people. *Quick, look over here, everyone, here's some mad shit, don't look in this direction where the real stuff is.* It's like when they dump bad news on the day of a disaster. I wouldn't be surprised if one day they trace the idea of putting funny photos of animals on the internet back to the FBI or something.

Being scared

I really like listening to scary stories on YouTube too, which I put down to being a fan of *Goosebumps* when I was a kid. I'll sit at work listening to scary (apparently) true stories and shitting myself up. I love the classic ones, like the one where someone phones someone and threatens to kill them and it turns out they're calling from inside their house, or the one everyone's heard where a man's head is being bounced on top of a car while his wife is sat inside not realizing (I know, I'm lovely).

I hate horror films but I still have to watch them. I have to make myself watch *Crimewatch* but I can't look out the window into the garden if it's dark, in case there's someone out there. Sometimes I'm even too scared to go to the toilet in the middle of the night when I've watched something that's freaked me out. I'll hold it in just in case a man with an axe is waiting in the hallway to chop me head off.

Me dad knows I get scared easily and he thinks he's *really* funny so he tries to frighten me. When I was about sixteen I had some friends round to watch *The Ring* and later that night my dad went into my room and pinned my hair extensions to one of my shelves. He added a raincoat and some boots underneath them so when I walked in my room it looked like the girl from *The Ring* was stood there. I've never been so scared in my entire life.

He also used to reach round from the bathroom window with a pole and tap on my bedroom window while I was in there. I was like, 'Why would you do that to me? I'm your first-born daughter and you're supposed to love me!'

Another time a bunch of my mates came round to watch a scary film and my parents tied an elephant keyring to a piece of string and put it under the table in the living room. As soon as the scary bit came on they pulled the keyring so it made a scraping noise across the floor and we absolutely shit ourselves. They thought it was the funniest thing ever. They were crying with laughter. We were just crying.

Me dad also used to pretend he was stuck down the plughole. He would hide behind the door in the bathroom. Me mam would come running in and say, 'Scarlett, come quick, he's done it again,' and he'd be doing this little voice from behind the door saying, 'Scarlett, I've fallen down, help me.' He also used to get house spiders and let them walk across his tongue so we wouldn't be scared of them. My dad leaves towels on the side of the bath so they can climb back out and he says, 'I'd rather have a house full of spiders than a house full of flies.' And I've said to him that in twenty-first-century Britain I think we've got other choices. It's not like the people who don't put towels in the bath are drowning in flies. It's like he sees the universe as this cosmic battle between spiders and flies and he's picked his side.

Aliens

I could talk about aliens for hours. Ever since I was little me dad and I have had a code word so that if an alien takes over our body and we're still inside there, we can try and scream out that word so we'd both know that an alien is impersonating us.*

When I was little I fell over on a plug and I had a triangle mark on my leg for a few hours, and me dad managed to convince me that I'd been probed. He said I was 'the chosen one', and even though I knew I'd fallen on a plug I kind of believed him.

I do believe in aliens and I'm always googling them and trying to do research. I think it's scarier to believe that it's just us here in this massive universe than it is to think that there are other people out there. It freaks me out to imagine we're all alone.

I don't think aliens have got big heads and long gangly fingers like ET, I think they're just like us. I wonder if some of them are actually already on earth. I see loads of people and think, *You're definitely not from this planet.* Sometimes when I see people who look like they could be from the cast of *The Hills Have Eyes* I do think, *What are you doing here? You should be in space somewhere.*

Maybe supermodels are aliens? A lot of them aren't conventionally pretty but you're sort of drawn to them, aren't you? And the ones that are stunning must also be aliens cos

---

* My editor wanted me to put the code word here but I told them, 'Then the aliens could read this and use it against me somehow.' I'm not stupid, me.

I don't think it's fair for people to be that good-looking other-wise.

Area 51

Area 51* fascinates me. Me dad and I are always watching programmes about it. You can't look at it on Google Images at all, which is so weird. I don't understand why people don't talk about it more. There's this whole place that exists that we're not allowed to know anything about and people are like, 'That's fair enough.' No, it's *not*! Why doesn't everyone want to know what goes on there? How can there be a whole place that's off limits that we don't know anything about? Why are they not telling us what's happening in there?

Maybe it's where the government people go to chill out where they know they won't be bothered? Perhaps it's actually full of loads of arcade games and slot machines? Maybe it's like Disneyland for the US government? If you were able to look at it on Google Maps, there'd just be all these pale government workers on lilos.

Zombie apocalypse

Me dad also thinks there's going to be a zombie apocalypse. He's got loads of tins of beans in the attic. He watches too much of *The Walking Dead*. He hasn't even got a tin opener up there. He said he'd bring one up. I can just imagine the zombie

---

* I have a friend who confuses it with Studio 54 and calls it Area 54. That'd be a nightclub full of people in suits and disco wigs.

apocalypse and us up in the attic gnawing at tins of beans. He's got old welding masks up there. I'm not sure what they'd be for. I think my dad sees himself as the leader in a zombie apocalypse. Me mam would probably volunteer to get bitten quite quickly just to escape the stress of it all. She'd probably like the camaraderie of being a zombie. Me and me dad and Ava would be walking across the countryside all tooled up with crossbows and axes. Dad buys apocalypse books. He'd be like Will Smith in *I Am Legend*, broadcasting through the *Gogglebox* cameras.

The thing is, round my way there'd be zombie ponies everywhere. Those Shetlands are horrible enough to begin with. I reckon you stick zombie teeth on a pony and it's going to be scary. London would be pretty horrible with the zombie pigeons as well. I don't think there's enough scenes with zombie animals in films.

Stunts and fails

I love watching videos of marriage proposals as well, but they make me cry so I have to be careful not to watch them if anyone's around.

What's mental is that YouTube has only been around for fifteen years. It feels like it's been a part of our lives forever. I can remember when it first started and it was just people singing songs who got famous. Some genuinely talented people have been discovered through it. Having said that, it also gives some people a reason to be stupid. You know when you see people jumping off roofs into dustbins and shit like that? I don't really get it. Once you've done that and put it on You-

Tube you'll always be known as the man who jumped from a roof into a dustbin. It's hardly something you want to put on your CV. I reckon there's people now who are leaders in their field and they go to present some big paper at a medical conference and everyone in the audience is like whispering to each other, 'Is that the one that jumped off a roof into a dustbin?'

And I like watching videos of fails too, when people are trying to do something like jump their bike over a ditch and they get it wrong and fall down. Basically what these videos prove is that it's never not funny to watch a skateboarder smash his testicles on a metal bar. I reckon that might be the greatest discovery of our generation. I also like the way that whatever the compilation and whatever else is in it, there's always a woman wearing a low-cut top so they can make that the image for the video. That's some sophisticated marketing right there.

Vloggers

One thing I really don't get is vloggers. I reckon they start off genuine but in no time they've got five million followers and they're making thousands of pounds a month from advertising and they're still, 'Ooh, you've caught me all unawares in my bedroom,' and I'm like, 'Your bedroom in your massive mansion, where you Scrooge McDuck about in all your money?' They remind me of the people that present Bid TV, or when you come in too late and switch the telly on and it's people betting on roulette and the person presenting it keeps mucking up their lines and stuttering. I don't understand it.

I'm from the generation that likes my TV presenters to be good at their jobs. And they're always like casually sipping Pepsi. 'Sorry guys, just drinking this delicious, nutritious beverage.' People aren't stupid, man.

It would be like me sitting down in front of *Gogglebox* and going, 'Ooh, this Domino's pizza is amazing,' because they're plying me with free ones (which they're not).*

I also worry that young girls are watching them and thinking they genuinely like those things they're talking about, and that they're being heavily influenced by what they recommend. I don't think vloggers are always very transparent about what they're promoting.

I've heard the government are bringing in loads of new rules for YouTubers and other vloggers and I think that's a really good thing. They've already started restricting what people can promote on Twitter. In the old days anyone could put a photo of themselves up hawking a product and they didn't have to admit they were being paid to do it, but now they have to put #spon after a post if that's the case. At least now people are aware that even if a celebrity is endorsing something, it may still be a load of old shit. I think it's only fair that everyone has to be more upfront. You need to be honest about what you flog while you vlog.

Mainly, though, I just think it's a shame that they've got this audience and they're making all this money and they're not actually saying that much a lot of the time. It's just like a constant Q and A with your sister's annoying mates. 'OK, so

---

* Dear Domino's, just so you know, I like ham and mushroom but don't even think about putting pineapple on me pizza. *shudders*

now I'm going to answer some of the questions you've sent in. What's your favourite colour? What kind of an animal would you be? What ice cream flavour do you like most?' 'Well, it's chocolate all the way.' Who's sitting up at night unable to sleep because they don't know what ice cream flavour someone would be?*

The one thing I really did like was when that Zoella talked about how to cope with anxiety, because that felt like someone using their fame to discuss something important and say that it's OK to admit that you have it. I think that probably did a load of good and it was really brave of her.

I think me not getting vlogging is another example of me being too old. But then my sister Ava watches them all and we watched one together the other day and even she was like, 'What's she on about?' I'm probably not watching the right ones or something.

But I guess I feel that happens a lot with stuff on the internet. It's like with the Icebox Challenge: how many people that did it really knew what it was for, and how many just thought it was a cool thing they could kind of show off about? It still raised loads of money, but then the internet moves on really quickly and everyone's gone back to dressing their pets up and stuff.

Dogs in outfits is never not funny, mind you.

---

* I'd obviously be something like toffee or mahogany flavour. You don't get enough wood-flavoured ice creams. Again, don't steal that, I reckon Duncan Bannatyne will be all over that.

Five things that confuse me

Google

Like, how does it know all of this stuff? You can literally type in 'quantum physics' and it comes up with a million results. It's so clever.

Gravity

I just don't get why people in the South Pole aren't walking around on their heads, because technically they are upside down. And wouldn't their heads get sucked into the middle of the world?

Insurance-company toys

Are there seriously people who choose their insurance based on what sort of toy they get given? Is there any bigger proof that no one understands what they're buying? Maybe it's just the most grown-up thing you can do is to get insurance, so you want to balance it out with something childish. What's next, toffee apples in solicitors' offices?

Fatty foods

Why do all fatty foods taste so nice yet they're bad for you? Why does something so tasty have so many downsides?

Life

Just in general. How it works, why we are here, what happens when we die? The whole thing completely baffles me, and what baffles me more is that no one really talks about it. It's like we forget how weird it is that we're walking around on this little planet, spinning round and round a big flaming star, while a little rock moon orbits around us. And everyone is popping babies out of their bits. What the actual eff is going on?

5

SCARLETT SAYS

. . . choose your clothes

Scarlett's Favourite Random Facts

Camels have three eyelids on each eye.

The largest snowflake ever recorded was 15 inches wide.

It rains diamonds on Jupiter and Saturn.

If I ever do get out of the bath, it's then time for me to choose my outfit.

I like to have at least three different looks set out on my bed because I never end up wearing the one that's in my head. It's always better in your imagination and then when you try it on you look like you're going to an office Christmas party. When you get a new outfit and you feel like you're the dog's bollocks, you have 'Daddy Cool' playing in your head. Then you wear it a second time and you don't feel as good. It wears off. You're always chasing that initial feeling. Having a new outfit is like heroin.*

To be fair, even though I spend days mulling over my outfit I always end up wearing the same thing anyway. If you look at my pictures on Facebook over a three-month period, it looks like I've been on a massive week-long bender in the same clothes.

I know what suits me now so I do have a bit of a uniform. I tend to wear jeans and a blazer because I think it looks smart but also quite casual. Obviously I have got several pairs of jeans and loads of blazers but people probably look at me and think, *She had that on last week, the scruffy bitch.* I'm like Bart

_____

* I say that as someone who's never even had a Pro Plus.

Simpson or Simon Cowell: I wear a variation of the same thing over and over. If it ain't broke, don't fix it, I say.

Even though I tend to stick to the same look there are still nights when I have a clothing nightmare. I'll spend ages staring into my wardrobe hoping some fucker from Narnia is going to appear from out the back of it and hand me something amazing to wear. I always say I've got nothing to wear but I've also got no space for any more clothes in my wardrobe so there's a bit of a disparity there.

I'll always check with my friends what they're wearing before I make any final decisions on my outfit. I also often get them to send me photos of what they're wearing so we don't end up in the same thing.

It's bad when that happens, and there are only so many shops to choose from so of course there's a crossover sometimes. If two people so want to wear the same thing, there always has to be that awkward conversation about which one is going to change. The other night Kelly and Sam both wore a black shift dress, a long chain necklace and their hair in loose waves. They were so similar they looked like the Chuckle Brothers, and they were standing next to each other in loads of photos so it was a bit ridiculous. People spent the whole night saying to them, 'You've both got the same outfit on!' as if they hadn't realized.

Squad goals

While me and my mates go out of our way to make sure we don't look the same, obviously there's this whole 'squad goals' thing that goes on where everyone dresses alike on purpose.

I saw a group of girls all wearing the colour mustard the other night and they'd obviously coordinated. Why? I wouldn't want to look like a shit version of Girls Aloud, thank you very much. It's like people decided it wasn't enough to dress in pink T-shirts with a nickname on once a year when they went to Magaluf and they wanted that fun all year round.

No jacket required

What I wear on a night out is never weather-dependent. Where I live you still see girls going out in summer dresses when it's snowing.

I'm a massive fan of online shopping, so that's where I get most of my clothes and accessories. It's just so much easier than *actual* shopping. You don't have to wait around in queues and search through rails for your size. You order what you want one day and it comes the next. It's like magic. When the package arrives I'm like, 'Yay!' because I forget that I've actually paid for it. If you don't physically have to hand over money, it's basically free, isn't it? It's like a mini Christmas every week in my house.

Tights

Glossy tights are one of my pet hates. I don't even know where people buy them? I just don't get the whole tights things anyway. And I really don't understand it when people wear tights with shorts. Surely it's one or the other? You'll end up sweaty and probably a little bit rashy. It's like sticking cling film round your legs and going out.

I think from the first day of autumn onwards you're legitimately allowed to wear tights, but you have to stop when it's spring again. Not old people – they can wear them anytime. But if you're not eligible for a free bus pass, tights when it's hot are *not* acceptable.

Local shopping

Where I'm from, the options are basically pound shops, nail parlours, charity shops and kebab shops.

Nail parlours

Before a certain point nail parlours didn't seem to exist and then suddenly they were everywhere. It's like they just invented another thing that we have to spend loads of time and money on. Before, you could just make sure your nails were a bit trimmed, a bit polished and that was enough. Now they have to be three-foot long, purple and shiny. And I don't understand what all these women who wear the masks were doing before. Were they just sitting at home being really good at putting fake nails on themselves but nobody ever asked them to do it for them? I feel like these shops appeared overnight.

Pound shops

When people refuse to shop in them, that's a real example of how some people will pay just to feel a little bit posher. 'You know next door in Poundland that shampoo is exactly the same but a pound?'*

There is a tiny part of me that wonders whether when I buy something from a pound shop I'm gonna get it home and the bottle's just going to be full of twigs and mud. Then someone came up with the 99p shop – that was a brilliant bit of branding, wasn't it? But then you pay 1p for the carrier bag, so it's actually a pound anyway. I refuse to go in the 99p shop, cos you've got to have your limits, haven't you? Otherwise, where does it end?

The high street

I do like high-street shopping but I find that a lot of the time when you go into shops the people who work there think they're mint. They're dressed like they're going for a night out at 11 a.m. I've worked in retail so I do understand what it's like. I worked in Topshop in York for a while and I know it's important to wear their clothes and try and make them look good, but you do not need to go to work wearing black lipstick with a fully contoured face. Calm the fuck down, man.

I used to work with a girl who definitely dressed better for work than she did for a night out and I never understood it.

---

* It's like people going mad over speedy boarding at the airport. They're just paying the extra money to feel a little bit special. You know the plane has to wait for everyone to get on before it can take off, right? And it's not like there aren't enough seats and some people have to go outside on the wing. It's literally just the people that want you to know they've paid a bit extra. It's a twat tax is what it is. Now, if they were like, pay £35 extra and you'll get an oxygen mask if the cabin pressure fails, then I'd pay it.

If I saw her out she looked quite scruffy, but she looked like she was going clubbing when she was behind the till. I also never understand why people go out shopping in skyscraper heels and dresses either. Seriously, put some flat shoes on. You're buying a top, not going clubbing. And I hate it when you ask a shop assistant for something in a different size and they look at you like you've just called their mother ugly. It's their job! If they can't be bothered to look out the back for it, they'll say, 'Sorry, everything's out on the shelves.' That is bollocks. They've got a massive storeroom they can't be arsed to sift through.

It also drives me mad – God, I'm right on one now – when the sales assistants are too busy having a laugh with each other to serve you. I actually saw two cashiers high-five each other the other day. WTAF?

takes a deep breath

Me mam describes my style as 'scruffy smart'. I've got really big boobs so I try to hide them. I always think I look really top heavy or slutty if I get them out. I generally buy the same things, so I'll have five tops or shirt dresses that are all ever so slightly different, to go with my identikit jeans and blazers. They all look the same but they may have a different print or cut that makes buying them acceptable.

You will never, ever see me in a bandage dress or some drapey shit with my boobs out. All my friends say that I dress like a MILF, which is weird because I don't have a kid, but I take it as a compliment.

One thing I'm really guilty of is buying whole outfits straight off the mannequin. Say if I walk past River Island and see something I like, I'll buy exactly what's on that mannequin. *Exactly.* Then I'll go out that night and see five other people who have done the same, and I'll have to spend the entire night dodging them. It's like the most embarrassing squad goals ever. #mannequinsquadgoals

Mannequins

Mannequins are so glamorous these days and most of them have better hair than me, which really pisses me off. They've got false eyelashes and everything. Back in the old days they were really square but now they're like style icons. Because there are so many cool ones, if I see one now that's got no head and arms I feel dead sorry for it. I'd love to know who gets to make the decision about whether or not they have nipples as well, cos some of them do and some of them don't. I wonder if you get to choose the nipples from a catalogue if you're the manager of the shop. I bet you'll be like me now and next time you go to Topshop, you'll check if they've got nipples.

There was a bit of an uproar about the size of mannequins recently, with people saying they're too thin, and I do get it. Everything looks good on a doll that's six foot tall and as thin as a pencil, but at the end of the day you're going to try that outfit on and people aren't stupid. Unless you are a supermodel or in serious denial no one actually thinks they look good in a leopard-print catsuit.

I've never understood why shops don't have smaller and curvier mannequins? I'd love that. Why not mix it up? Someone is missing a trick not making variations. It would make things a bit more interesting. Some clothes actually look better on people who are shorter or have boobs, so why not put them on a mannequin they'd suit?

I do find it ridiculous that shops have size-zero mannequins representing all of their clothes. It feels so old-fashioned. I think one day we'll look back and be really shocked that there was only one kind of mannequin. It'll be a bit like the smoking ban, and how we've all forgotten what it was like when people could smoke in restaurants and even on planes. You won't remember what the world was like before there were mannequins of all shapes and sizes and colours. I really hope that happens anyway. They could start with a bit more of a normal-sized one in the meantime at least.

While we're on the subject, I do get a bit pissed off with online shopping when stores have plus-size models that don't look like they're in any way plus size. Why don't they put the outfit on someone's who's got a bigger bum so you can actually see how it fits? Wouldn't that be novel? Maybe we'd all stop feeling like the world wants us to be lamp posts in wigs.

I hate it when I go shopping and I'm made to feel uncomfortable because I've asked for something in a bigger size. I've been properly looked up and down before because I'm not a size 6. How dare I ask for something in a size that will actually fit my boobs! I'm not just being paranoid; I do feel like I'm judged sometimes.

My friend Sam put as her Facebook status once, 'I was the lucky fat girl today. I managed to get something in a size 16!' She always says that there will only be one curvy girl who gets lucky on a Saturday afternoon because shops will only ever have one of each item of clothing in a bigger size.

There will be rails of smaller sizes and everyone will be

knocking each other out the way with their handbags to get the one bigger size. It's like shops are ashamed to stock things above a 12 when statistically more women in the country are a size 16 than any other size. What do they expect them to wear?

I bet there was a point back in the day when all of the shops realized that all they had to do was make us feel really shit about ourselves and we'd buy more clothes to make ourselves feel better. So they made sure literally no one would ever look the same shape as the mannequins. And then the magazines were like, 'Ooh, I think we could help with making women feel like shit too.' So we had like fifty years of that. And now they don't even have to pay people upfront, they've got people volunteering to take photos of themselves on Instagram that make us all feel really shit about the way we look. And that, ladies and gentlemen, is the definition of progress. Although I'm sure we probably all feel like this no matter what shape and size we are.

I went to see Nicky Minaj in concert last year. She did the talky-shouty voice thing. My mate thought she was possessed. She did that song where she insulted skinny bitches and I was like, 'You're skinny, you just have a big implanted arse.'

I feel like people can't win when it comes to the whole body-shaming thing. I felt dead sorry for Cheryl* when everyone was commenting on her losing weight. You're either too fat or you're too thin. Can the media please print exactly how they think everyone should look so we can make sure we adhere to the rules?

---

* I've been a bit left behind with what her surname is.

One minute someone is too big, the next they're too small. It's almost worse when women body-shame other women. I've been asked to do so many interviews about weight loss for magazines, and some have even said they'll pay me to lose weight for a feature. WTF? Never in a million years.

We're all different so there is no such thing as the right shape. In fact, there is. Your shape is the right shape, whatever shape that is.

It's like when a newspaper does a story about an actress at a premiere or something and they're like, 'So and so was flaunting her shoulders last night,' and they're literally just standing there, in a dress. It's true they've got shoulders but my English teacher must have taught me a different definition of 'flaunting' because I didn't think it meant that.

Solo shopping

With all the stress of being in a shop, I can't be arsed to wait around while everyone tries on ten tops. People think I'm weird but I would much rather go shopping on my own than with my mates. I refuse to go shopping with the girls. They'll have shopping days out and when they invite me I'm like, 'Nah, I'm all right.' I can't be arsed with fannying around. I'm also too easily influenced. I'll try something on and think it's minging and before I know it I'll be at the till paying for it because they've all convinced me it looks great. Then I get it home and realize I was right all along and have to go through the pain of taking it back.

I'm definitely a loner when it comes to shopping, but I don't mind going with me mam because that's different. She's always totally honest with me and she gets shit done. She's like, 'Try it on, buy it or leave.' I like that kind of no-nonsense shopping attitude. She's like the Terminator of shopping buddies.

Designer clothes

My mates and I love it when we get a bargain. We're all like, 'Guess how much this was? It was *dead* cheap!'

It's nice having nice things, but I would never spend hundreds of pounds on a top. I stop wearing things as soon as they start reappearing on my Facebook page so I'd rather buy things I don't feel too guilty about not wearing again.

My friend loves Vivienne Westwood and it's not even that expensive but I still wouldn't spend £70 on a T-shirt when you can buy one from Primark for £1.50. People only do it so they can say, 'It's so and so.' I don't even know who half of the designers are to be honest, and I don't care. It's not like I'm going to be begging an outfit off them for the Oscars any time soon.

The ten last things I bought

1) A cinema ticket

2) Caramel popcorn and a large ice blast

3) A blow-dry at Truly Scrumptious in Bishop Auckland

4) A shirt dress from River Island

5) A Mac lipstick in Velvet Teddy

6 A Toshiba laptop

7) A Jacqueline Wilson magazine for my little sister

8) Fake Bake darker spray tan

9) Two Pornstar Martinis from Fat Buddha in Durham

10) Five pairs of false eyelashes

Tantastic

Once the outfit decision has been made, I can get on with everything else.

The most important part for me has already started, though.

OK, it's not exactly a secret that I *love* fake tan. Probably more than most of my friends. In fact, some of my mates don't even wear it, and they really suit the natural look, but it creates a lot of problems when we take photos on a night out. It's really difficult to find a filter where I don't look like I'm an incredibly weird colour.

My friend took a picture recently where I looked like Piccadilly because of the filter she used. No, hang on, it's piccalilli, isn't it? She said it was the only filter where I didn't look green; so instead I looked luminous yellow.

Some of my friends don't like me staying over at their house after a night out because of my fake tan. If I stay at Kelly's, she gets really upset because I leave a tan outline of my body on her bed sheet that looks like one of those chalk drawings you get when someone's been murdered.

I get told off by me mam all the time for leaving fake tan on our bathroom floor. I always put a towel down but I often miss a bit, and the amount of times me mam's slipped over is ridiculous. I'll just hear a thud and then a really loud, 'SCARLETT!' It makes me laugh so much. All of my family have got permanently tanned soles of their feet, and the bathroom door is kind of a mottled brown colour now, so that's starting to get a tan too. But Ava does all right out of it. I pay her to do my back now she's old enough, and sometimes if she's feeling cheeky she'll charge me a bloody fiver for it because she knows I have no choice. She's like a mini Alan Sugar with a tanning mitt.

I also get her to dry my hair for me sometimes so I can get on with doing my make-up to save time. She doesn't style it or anything, she literally just dries it, but needless to say she charges for that too . . .

One day I went to work without any fake tan on and people kept asking me if I was ill. I've got really fair skin and really dark hair so I looked like a pale goth. I'm genuinely almost see-through and my veins glow as if they're under UV lighting so I do look really different. Everyone was so confused and I was saying to them, 'This is my actual skin. This is just what I look like.' I think I'm going to have to wear fake tan forever now. I'm going to be a very orange ninety-year-old.

Me mam used to put fake tan on a plate and then use a mini paint roller to apply it on me. It lasted for bloody days. My school uniform consisted of a yellow shirt and pale blue jumper, so you can imagine how dark I looked wearing that. I think it's the reason I didn't win any dancing awards until I was about twelve. I probably looked absolutely fucking terrifying.

I used to use this gold Rimmel powder me mam bought me as well, and my nanny's got this massive portrait of me on her wall from my dancing days where I've got a monobrow, fake eyelashes and a face like the sun. I looked like one of those people who dresses up as a gold statue and stands in Covent Garden trying to get money out of tourists. The best thing is that I'm wearing a yellow dress in the photo and she's put it in a gold frame. She doesn't need to put any lights on in her hallway because that picture literally glows. She could put them up all over her house and save a fortune on electricity.

I think when you start wearing fake tan you have to be in it for the long haul and be prepared to put in the hours and have the right tools. You've got to dedicate a night to exfoliating and moisturizing, and then get up in the morning to do the actual tan. You've got to have at least one spare mitt just in case as well. I used to use a bloody sock to put me tan on!

I would now honestly rather go out with old fake tan on than no fake tan on. You know when your tan is a few days old it can go a bit green? I would rather top that up and go out looking like Shrek than take the whole lot off and go out looking like Casper.

Sometimes my skin goes really patchy and I look like I've got a skin disease, and that's when I know I have to completely start over again. I have to go right back to the beginning and redo the entire routine, but it's worth it. It's like painting the Forth Bridge. Honestly, it's like my hobby.

Essex

I feel as if Essex is the place I'd have to live if I ever moved down south. No one wears fake tan in London, so Essex is the only place that I'd be accepted as part of the fake-tanned community. Although I probably wouldn't be able to understand a word anyone was saying and vice versa. We'd need a phrasebook to translate.

I was reading the other day that experts are starting to find out about the negative effects of fake tan. Apparently it can cause mood swings so I'm going to use it as an excuse now whenever I feel shit. 'It's not me being moody, it's the tan talking.'

Ballroom dancing

I started wearing fake tan properly, out of choice, when I was thirteen. But I wore it from an even younger age because I did a lot of ballroom dancing, so I was a pretty early starter.

I was five when I started ballroom dancing but I didn't start competing until I was six. I loved it but unfortunately it was in the pre-*Strictly Come Dancing* days so everyone used to take the mickey out of how old-fashioned it was.

I carried on dancing until I was twenty-one. The first nine years everyone was all 'Why do you do old-people dancing?' When I won awards and I'd be in the local paper, kids at school would make comments about it being old people dancing, so it was such a relief when *Strictly* started because people got interested in it and it became 'cool', and some were actually really impressed.

But before then my life was basically the plot of a very low-budget version of one of those *Step Up* films. Ballroom dancing was so uncool back then that I knew a boy who changed his name when he danced so people in his area didn't know it was him. Another guy I knew pretended his trophies were for drumming.

Going to the Blackpool ballroom was always the highlight of my year. I used to think it was magical when the piano player came up from underneath the floor.*

I think dancing helped to make me confident. You dance with someone really closely and you have to make a lot of eye contact, and even now I'm never scared of looking in people's eyes when I speak to them. Some people will look everywhere but at you when you're having a conversation, and I probably come across as quite scary because I don't take my eyes off people. Sometimes I have to make myself look away and then look back so I don't seem like a serial killer.

I'd love to go on *Strictly* but I just don't think they'd let me on. I'm basically a ringer, as I've danced against some of the professionals in competitions when I was younger.

I stopped ballroom dancing about five years ago because it took up so much of my time, but I used to go to competitions in Portugal and Paris, and I've won national titles. I was trained by Anton du Beke from *Strictly* back in the day. He's such a lovely man.

---

* I took our Ava there recently and she thought it was shit. I tried to get her excited: 'He's coming from the floor.' And she was just like, 'Yeah, on a machine.' I took her to the Illuminations too, and she just looked at it and said, 'What a waste of electricity.' I tell you, man, that generation, they're a tough crowd.

I watch it now and I do have a slightly different take on the show. I'll be watching someone dance and I'll say, 'He had no rise and fall and no lilt,' and my dad will look at me like I'm mental and then Len Goodman will comment and he'll say exactly the same thing.

Me little snippet of wisdom on the subject: people with glasses tend to be shit dancers. It's just physics. The laws of physics.

Tanorexia

I reckon the newspapers tried to make this a thing when it wasn't. They found one woman who did it and they were like, 'Tanorexia is sweeping the country.' And I reckon they were basically just really proud of the pun. That woman was an amazing colour, though.

Round our end, people started taking these pills and injecting themselves with this stuff that made you get a tan. Everyone I knew was doing it. It gave them a tan but it was giving them really bad migraines. And there were loads of people doing it.

I remember when that orange juice Sunny Delight was massive years ago and there was this news story that did the rounds saying that it was turning people orange. I can remember drinking so much Sunny D so I'd look tanned. It didn't work, though, so that's how I can say with absolute confidence: that story was bollocks.

Hair

The second most important part of my night out preparations is my hair. If I'm going out on a Friday night, I'll wash and blow-dry my hair in the morning before work so that I can do it quickly when I get in, otherwise it would add another hour on to my prep.

If we're off out on a Saturday, it becomes a part of my day-long prep. I've got really thick hair *and* hair extensions, so it takes forever to dry – sometimes up to an hour and a half! That's why I have to plan ahead and rope Ava in to help, at great expense.

I think it's a northern thing but when I was at school I used to wrap my fringe around a Coca Cola can and hairspray if for about twenty seconds so it formed a big roll, and then I'd scrape the rest of my hair back. It would be so much easier if I could do that now and not look like a total twat.

In fact, I went through a real chav stage when I was thirteen. As I've said, I was a funny-looking kid but I always dressed nice and had heels and nice dresses and that, but when I got to thirteen I decided I wanted to be a chav to fit in. Everyone has that stage. So I made me mam buy me loads of Fred Perry stuff and threw out me heels. Lots of England shirts and denim skirts and Nike Air Max, which are now cool in a retro way. I had the tracksuits with poppers on the legs. Thinking about it now, I'm not really sure why there were poppers. Maybe to make them into flares if you wanted?

I literally based my style on Vicky Pollard from *Little Britain*. I remember watching an episode when she had loads of scrunchies in her hair and she was like, 'That's how many

people I've had a fight with.' And I went in the next day and wore loads of scrunchies to make myself look hard. That lasted three months and then I came to my senses.

The hairdryer

If I'm feeling a bit flashy at the weekend, I may go to the hairdresser's and get a proper blow-dry on a Saturday morning. But generally I'll do it myself, which drives me dad mad because he moans about all the hair in the sink. He says it looks like a monkey has had a shave in the basin.

I love having long hair but it's such an effort. By the time I've finished doing it I feel like I've been to the gym and done a proper workout. My arms really ache and I'll have a right sweat on. I once sweated so much while I was trying to blow-dry my hair I had to have another shower wearing a massive shower cap before I could get dressed.

It doesn't help that my bedroom is like a bloody Harry Potter cupboard. I've got the worst bedroom in the house because it's tiny, so if someone walks in after I've been using my hairdryer they get whacked in the face by the heat. It's like that feeling when you get off a plane when you go on holiday and feel like you're being beaten around the face by the humidity.

The tiny bedroom

I'm so cross about the utter shitness of my room. Back in the days when I was the favourite child, before our Ava came along, I had the biggest bedroom *and* the little room I'm in now just to watch TV in. I was really spoilt.

Even in our old house I had two rooms – my lilac room and my animal room – but I get none of that now. When Ava was born I got demoted to the second biggest bedroom in the house because my parents needed the big room to put the cot in, and then when Ava was old enough she moved into the little room.

Then I went away to uni, which was a big mistake, because when I came back I'd been moved into the tiny cupboard room and Ava had taken over my bedroom. I walked in and I was like, 'Where's all my stuff?' and then found it squeezed into the cubbyhole. Gutted.

I feel like Alice in Wonderland when I'm in that bedroom. You know that bit where her arms and legs are poking out of windows? That's me when I try to go to bed. The room is a weird shape as well, so I have to jump over my bed to get to my things. I don't need to be doing an assault course before a night out. Not after all the effort of doing my hair.

Even though my bedroom is tiny, Ava will only dry my hair in there because I'm not allowed in hers. She's got a sign on the door that says 'No Scarletts allowed'. I don't know why; it's not like I'm nasty to her or anything. I asked her the other day why she won't let anyone in there and she said it's because she needs her own space. She's not even ten.

It's no wonder she wants to stay in there, though. She's got Netflix and Sky Plus to enjoy and I don't even have bloody Freeview. I've been totally demoted. I feel like a second-class citizen in my own home. If I was on the *Titanic*, I'd have been right below deck playing banjo with all the Irish people, and me mam, dad and Ava would have been sitting up in the Palm Court having dinner with the captain.

Sky Plus

I still can't get my head around the idea that you can pause telly. Sometimes I forget when you're watching live and I get frustrated that you can't fast-forward into the future. When I was little I used to line up all my video boxes and pretend I was Dorothy on the yellow brick road. And when I had a hamster I made him these amazing mazes out of all of them, too. And I was telling Ava about that and she was like, 'What is a video?' So I told her it's a big square thing with one film on it. Then I started telling her about going to Woolworths to get tapes to record music off the radio. She looked at me like I was an old lady from the past. Fair dos, she's got better technology, but she'll never know the joy of pick'n'mix from Woolworths.

Music

I was talking to my sister about sharing headphones on a DC Discman player the other day and I may as well have been talking about gramophones. I was fourteen when I got an iPod. You look at it now and it looks massive, it was so chunky. Me dad was all about minidiscs. He thought they were the future. But nowadays your phone basically has every song ever on it, doesn't it?

I remember, at university, when everyone would be downloading music and videos. It's stealing, obviously, but everyone did it.

I also remember you used to be able to send music via Bluetooth on your phone and you'd have to put your phones really close together, and I remember when everyone had the same phone and played Snake. And I had this thing on my phone that you could design your own ringtone with and I thought I was a music producer with all these weird bleepy noises for a ringtone. I thought I was David Guetta. I remember running home from school so I could get on MSN before my mam would call my nanny. And if you timed it wrong, she'd be like, 'Get off the internet, I'm on the phone.' And it'd make that weird screeching noise when it was dialling up.

You'd keep logging off and on MSN Messenger so you'd pop up on someone's screen and they'd notice you. Or you'd put a song lyric as your name. It was dead embarrassing.

I think it's a massive problem because it's good to be able to wait for things you want. Nowadays everything happens instantly and we're all basically spoilt brats. You should see what people get like if the free Wi-Fi stops working in a cafe somewhere. People are genuinely like they've had something stolen from them. You can't go back from that, can you?

Hair extensions

Even though I moan about doing my hair, I do like it, and in my opinion bigger is better.

I first started wearing hair extensions when I was fifteen. Although calling them hair extensions is pushing it a bit. They were basically these long, straggly clip-ins that looked like I'd fashioned them from what I'd found on the floor of a hairdresser's. In one of my school photos I've got really thick, shoulder-length hair and then just two long, thin clip-ins attached to the back so it looks like I've got a mullet.

I started to get proper bonded extensions when I was about twenty, when I was halfway through uni. Obviously I made sure I spent my student loan on something worthwhile.

I've pretty much always had long hair, and I do quite like the fake look. I don't mean like Jodie Marsh fake, but I like everything to be a bit over the top. About half of my friends are really natural, and the other half have big extensions like me, so about 90 per cent of our selfies are hair. We all look like we're standing next to Cousin Itt.

I've had some really bad hairstyles in my time. If you want to see them, you can skip to the middle of the book. I once had traffic-light-red hair so I looked like a wrestler, and I also had really dark hair with a blonde quiff. Who *does* that? My hair was really dark and just my fringe had blonde highlights in it. I mean, how did I ever think that was OK? I'm disgusted at myself.

When I was nineteen I decided I wanted to be mature and have a bob for a bit of a change, but as soon as I got my hair cut I cried my eyes out. It didn't suit my big moon face in any way. You know how usually when you have quite a dramatic haircut everyone says it looks lovely? Not one person did. *No one.* Even me mam and dad didn't comment, and when I pushed them all they said was, 'Ooh, it's different, isn't it?'

The final straw was when my boyfriend at the time came to pick me up and he took one look at me and said, 'What the

hell have you done to your hair?' I went straight out that day and bought some expensive clip-in hair extensions. Me and short hair will never be friends.

Me mam's always had really, really long hair. But one day she got this crop and she looked like Action Man. She was that unhappy with it she said she was driving to the viaduct.

Top ten hairdressers with puns for names

1) Sheerlock Combs

2) British Hairways

3) Hairway to Heaven

4) Crops and Bobbers

5) Hair2Eternity

6) Headonizm

7) Hair Today Gone Tomorrow

8) Curl Up and Dye

9) The God Barber

10) Do or Dye

A brief interlude on body hair

Body hair seems to be a massive feminist issue, and of course women should be able to grow it long and plait it if they want to. But personally I've got a bit of a phobia about it. I even wax my arms. I think it's partly because having smooth skin is better when it comes to fake-tanning, so I whip it all off.

Obviously it's totally up to women what they want to do when it comes to their own body hair, but I always shave my armpit hair if I'm wearing something sleeveless. I don't think it looks that nice when people grow their armpit hair and dye it like Miley Cyrus does. I'm all for growing my leg hair in winter because it keeps you warm, but I think your under-arms are different. Sometimes my leg hair grows so long it looks like I'm wearing leggings when I'm not, but it's cosy. That's totally illogical, isn't it? That's the thing, it's either all off, or all on. But I still feel like it's different. I think.

Vajazzles?

In general, I think people can do what they want in their pants: if they like that vintage 70s look, then go for it; if they want a Bounty bar down there, then that's fine too. People should do whatever they feel comfortable with. Let it all hang out. But I do think there's something a bit weird about gluing jewels to your fanny. It's like bribing someone to go near it. 'I know it's disgusting but I'm trying my best.' It's like on the TV where they advertise a special spray for freshening up 'down there'. If you feel like that's something you want to do, go for it. But the danger is that someone starts feeling like it makes them a dirty cow if they don't do it. I guess there's only a finite amount of armpits on the planet, but if you can convince half the world's population they need to buy a whole extra deodorant, that's a lot of money, isn't it? It does feel like another one of these things where people have got together and decided how best to make women feel like shit. 'Don't worry, they'll spend so long spraying and gluing jewels to their fannies they'll never have time to take over the world.'

One thing I don't like is the way men shave all of their hair off these days. I don't understand why a man will spend months and months growing a beard but then shave everything else off from his chin down. I like it when men have shirts on and you can see a bit of hair poking out, but these days a lot of men like to look smooth as an otter.

I don't mind men shaving their backs if they've got a pubey back, though. In fact, I'd encourage it. You can definitely see that we've descended from apes when you see a man with a really hairy back.

Make-up

So once hair is done, it's time for make-up, which also takes so bloody long to do. And I'm not going to lie: I do wear a *lot* of make-up when I'm going out.

Make-up always comes after I've done my hair (or during if I'm paying our Ava half my wages to dry it) and because of that I often end up with foundation in my hairline. I spend ages trying to get it out with a baby wipe and then end up applying a ton more anyway.

When I get all of the products I put on my face out of my make-up bag and lay them on the floor ready, it really is ridiculous. I genuinely can't believe my face can breathe underneath all of it. One day I'm going to die and it will be death by cosmetics. I'll be like that woman in *Goldfinger* who suffocates because she's covered in gold paint. The thing is, I do know it's all bollocks. With my rational brain, I know that I don't need more make-up. But then there'll be an advert on the telly and they'll be like, 'Voted product of the year by readers of slapface magazine' and I'll be like, 'Ooh, that sounds good.' I think it's the closest I get to understanding drugs. You just can't control yourself. I don't fall for all that science stuff with the skin creams, though, where they're like, 'Made with new fluoro nanocarbon fruit peptide anti-ageing technology'. It's the same old bloop it always is, man.

Contouring

The Kardashians have got a lot to answer for. In the old days you could put a bit of lip gloss on, some bronzer and you were away. But now you basically have to draw a whole new face on.

The other day I was sat in the living room doing my contouring because there's better lighting in there, and when me dad walked in he said, 'Are you going to a fancy dress party? You look like a tribal warrior.' To be fair, he was spot on.

I like the contouring trend but sometimes people take it a bit too far and they look like they've got a beard or sideburns. When I search #contour on Instagram some of it is so extreme people look like different human beings. Some people look great in photos and like they've got their application down to a fine art, and then you see them in person and they look like werewolves.

I can do my make-up in an hour, if I don't get distracted

by the phone or TV, but by the time I've moisturized, prepped, primered, put on foundation, contoured with cream, added concealer, bronzer, more primer, contouring powder, primer and blusher – and that's before I do my eyes, eyebrows and lipstick – I basically look like a totally different person.

I think I unintentionally catfish people on Instagram. Me mam always tells me I look miles better in photos like it's a compliment. It's one thing saying someone is photogenic, but it's another saying that the picture version of them is far better than the real thing. I'd much rather look shit in photos and better in real life so people are pleasantly surprised.

I reckon if someone who didn't know me looked at my photos and then met me they'd be like, 'Who's that person in the photos, because it isn't you?' I showed my little sister a picture of me on a night out a while back and she said, 'Who's that woman?' When I said it was me she replied, 'But you don't look that nice in real life, Scarlett.' Thanks Ava.

I actually thought the photo that Kim Kardashian posted of her in the middle of contouring was a really good thing. If you didn't see that type of thing, then you wouldn't realize the amount of time that goes into making people look the way they do. I really liked that girl recently who came out and told everyone the amount of time she spent trying to look as good as she did in her photos. She spent the whole day taking one photo and pretending it was casual. She also told everyone how she hadn't eaten all day beforehand and was sucking her stomach in to make herself look the way she did. There are people that pretend it's so effortless and I think that's wrong. It makes people feel like there must be something wrong with them if they don't look like all those beautiful women in the

magazines. Like the no-make-up selfie thing. All those models looking amazing, pretending they'd just woken up. It's like the old trick of waking up early and brushing your teeth the first night you stay over at someone's house, so they think you don't get morning breath.

Make-up fails

I've had so many make-up fails in my life, so these days I don't take any chances. If I need to stock up or I want to change my look slightly, I'll go into a department store, ask them to make my face four times darker than it really is, and do the rest of my make-up. Then I buy everything they use. It's so much easier than guess work. I trust them not to make me look like I'm having a massive make-up malfunction. I've definitely had a few of those over the years. I went through a phase of wearing jet-black eyeshadow with pink and orange eye shadow and pink lipstick. I looked like a drag queen Power Ranger. I'm surprised I didn't get snapped as a 'before' picture for a makeover advert.

Eyebrows

I didn't used to know about eyebrow pencils, so I would use eyeliner to draw me eyebrows in. I looked like one of those mad old ladies you see on the high street. One thing I am pleased about is that for the first time in my life I can say I know how to do my eyebrows properly. Over the years I've done everything from the upside down Nike tick to the giant slug and I feel like I'm finally happy with the shape of them.

I always make sure I get my eyebrows threaded at least three days before I'm going out to give them time to calm down. I go to this salon near my house to get them done and every time I go in they ask me if I want my upper lip doing at the same time. I give them such a look. Surely I would ask if I wanted that done too? I've started to get paranoid I look like a moustached hipster without realizing it.

Lips

I know overly outlining your lips has become really popular and I have tried it, but whenever I take selfies I look like Pete Burns. People put up tutorials on YouTube and they always look really good, but I can't do it at all. The thing is, everyone tries to look like Kylie Jenner but they go way over the top. I'm saying that as if Kylie Jenner *hasn't* gone way over the top.

Surgery

I'm not against anyone having stuff done to themselves if it makes them happier, and I've dabbled, but I do think seventeen was way too young for Kylie to have had her lips plumped. I do worry that so much emphasis is put on what we look like now and there's so much pressure to have Botox and everything. Back when it first started it was mainly older people who had the minor surgery stuff done, but now girls of my age and younger are getting Botox and collagen injections. It's all gone a bit crazy.

Like I said before, I think if surgery or procedures make people feel better about themselves, then fair enough. I get lip fillers because my top lip is non-existent, so I would be hypo-critical if I judged anyone else. I started getting mine done when I was about twenty, so, long before *Gogglebox*, and I've had veneers on my teeth too, because it was always something I wanted to get done.

I can stand here and say it's my choice, but then am I only making that choice because of pressures from outside? Unfor-tunately we live in a very appearance-oriented society and being on telly has made me more conscious of how I look. Me mam is such a strong person and even she's contemplating getting Botox because a few people have said nasty things on Twitter. But it's nothing these days, is it? Everyone does it. I do sometimes wonder what they'll think in the future, though. 'You took some neurotoxin from bacteria, and injected it in your face?' It'll be like when we look back and people were painting their faces with lead to look pale. I reckon even if you went back to prehistoric times there would still have been people doing things to themselves to make themselves look different, so it must just be something in us.*

I would be nervous about having Botox because I've had Bell's palsy and there's a danger one side of my face would droop, but I'd like to have my breasts lifted at some point. I've got big boobs and I'm only twenty-five and they're already starting to clean my shoes so I really do think I'd do it.

I believe it's important to do it for yourself and no one else,

---

* It's in the Bible too, isn't it? The apple that made everyone ashamed of their nakedness. Everyone blames Eve, but to be fair, it sounds like she was off her face at the time. 'Eve, why did you eat that apple?' 'Talking snake told me to.' Riiiiiight.

though. I want to be able to look in the mirror and feel happy. If surgery makes you feel a bit more confident, then why not?

But one thing I would say is make sure you research who you go to see because there are some really dodgy people out there who aren't properly qualified. I had a bit of a disaster once where someone put too much lip filler in and I looked ridiculous. I couldn't leave the house for about three days and I honestly thought I was going to spend the rest of my life looking like a camel.

6
SCARLETT SAYS

. . . cheers!

Scarlett's Favourite Random Facts

Each person uses an average of fifty-seven sheets of toilet paper per day.

More Monopoly money than real money is printed in the world each year.

Crocodiles can't stick their tongues out.

First(ish) drink of the night

While I'm getting ready at home I'll have my first drink of the evening. It's usually a glass of red wine, but I never have a second one because I get drunk quite easily and I don't want to be putting my make-up on badly and looking a state, do I? But by the time I get to pre-pre-drinks, I'm ready to go.

This generally involves us sitting around someone's kitchen or living room drinking and talking crap. I like going to Kelly's parents' house because they've got an open-plan living room and kitchen so we've got loads of room. Her poor parents go and sit upstairs out of the way, bless them, and I do feel bad for them. If we go to Sarah's house, we've got the run of the place because she lives on her own, so I like it there too. But as long as we're all together, drinking anywhere is mint.

Who I'd invite to my dream dinner party

Jesus
It would be a cheap night for booze because I could just bring loads of buckets of water to the table and he could

turn them into wine. I wonder if you'd be able to put an order in for what you want? Like, 'Can I have a glass of Sauvignon Blanc or a Zinfandel?' Or would you just have to drink what you're given?

Houdini
It would be funny because I think him and Jesus would try and outdo each other, like, 'I can escape out of this.' 'I once healed a leper.'

Mary Berry
Who doesn't love Mary Berry? She would be full of cookery innuendos and she could help me make the dessert.

Boris Johnson
The man is a hoot. I would ask him what his views on aliens are and what he really thinks of David Cameron.

Prince Harry
I'll make sure he realizes it isn't fancy dress. We don't want any Nazi surprises. I'd get some cards in because I've heard he's a dab hand at strip poker.

Alan Carr
He's very funny and he likes random booze, so he can make Mary Berry do some weird shots.

Vicky Pattison
Fellow north-easterner. Absolutely mint and so clever. Also, wouldn't take any shit from Houdini.

Johnny Depp

I'd like Johnny to come but I'd request he came as Edward Scissorhands for two reasons: 1) so he can cut up the meat, and 2) because it would be funny as fuck to watch him try and eat peas.

Timekeeping

Actually leaving the house on time is *so* hard for me and I'm generally half an hour late everywhere I go. My friends have got clever about my bad timekeeping now, and if they want me to be somewhere at 9 p.m. they'll tell me I have to be there at 8.30 p.m. so I've got a buffer.

I don't know why I'm always late, I really don't. I just don't seem to be able to help myself. My friends will phone and say, 'Are you nearly ready?' and I'll be like, 'Yeah, I am actually!' while I'm sat there in my pyjamas. I desperately want to be on time, or even early, but it never happens.

My God, can you imagine turning up somewhere early? I can't. My friends hate my shit timekeeping and I know how annoying it is but it's like a habit I can't seem to break.

I really don't understand people who are always on time. I seem to be forever fannying about and, before I know it, hours have passed. I'll tell myself I'll have a 'quick' bath, I'll read a magazine and watch videos on YouTube, and all of a sudden I'll realize I'm freezing cold and I have to top the hot water up. Another forty-five minutes later I'm still in there pretending I'm a mermaid. I love mermaids and I think part of the reason I have long hair is so I can feel a bit mermaidy. I was obsessed with *The Little Mermaid* when I was kid and it's never really worn off. At the time I think I just really liked her long hair and the fact she had a shell bra, which seemed so cool. But now when I think about it, she gave up the most important things in her life – all her friends and everything that made her happy – for a lad. And just think about him for a minute. He liked her and she couldn't speak. And she didn't have any legs. So he basically liked her for the top half of her body and that alone. What a dick. And she was all, 'He likes me, he likes me! I'm leaving the sea.' Me and my mates talked for ages about what should have happened at the end of the film, and decided that when she changes she should get the head of a fish and human legs and genitals. That'd teach him. Although knowing the kind of dickhead he clearly is, he'd be all, 'You don't need to look at the mantelpiece when you're poking the fire. I'll hop on.'

But still, who wouldn't want a Jamaican crab for a friend?

Making an entrance

I also genuinely think that part of the reason I'm late to the pre-pre-drinks is because I like walking in somewhere when all my friends are already there. Because they'll have had some drinks so I get a bigger reception. I feel like I'm a bit of a novelty because they've already had about an hour of catching up with each other and I'm fresh entertainment. It's basically a really sneaky way of being the headliner on a night out.

I never ask me dad what I look like before I go out because he always goes, 'You've got far too much make-up on.' But then if he didn't say that, I'd know I hadn't done the job

properly and I'd put more on. I'll always put another lot of bronzer on right before I leave the house just in case anyway, but if my dad doesn't think I look orange enough I'll ramp it up.

Me mam is my benchmark when it comes to my outfits and I know that if I ask her how I look I'll be able to work out if I look good or not. She's got quite an obvious code. If she says I look 'nice', 'OK' or 'all right', I'll change. No one wants to be told they look 'all right' after spending five hours getting ready, do they?

If I'm wearing a shirt dress, I'll often put jeans on underneath and then take them off when I get to one of my friends' houses because otherwise me dad will say it's too short. He doesn't have Facebook so he'll never know I've done a sneaky change later in the evening.*

Once I'm *finally* ready to go out I head straight to one of my mates' places. I rarely have the girls round to mine before a night out because I don't like everyone drinking around my little sister (that also means I never have to clear up the following day with a minging hangover).

Usually one of my friends will come and pick me up and give me a lift, or I'll subtly say to me mam, 'Have you got a taxi number?' and wait for her to offer to take me. We both know it's a bit of a game and sometimes she doesn't play along so I'll pretend to call a taxi. I won't actually ring the number but I'll make out I'm having a conversation with someone until she feels guilty and caves in. It's so weird. We both know we're being twats but we still do it.

---

* Dad, if you're reading this, it's a joke. I often wear jeans out to nightclubs.

We all take our own alcohol but we'll share mixers, and whoever is hosting usually gets some crisps and things in. Kelly will make proper nibbles and put plastic cups on the table. She's a really good host, unlike me. If ever people do come to mine, I don't organize anything. They're lucky if they get something to drink their booze out of, let alone some Kettle Chips.

Early drinking days

I had my first ever drink at the age of ten, and it was my granddad Tommy's fault. I asked him for a mocktail with sparklers and umbrellas. I drank half of it and apparently I started being really loud and stuff. It turned out it was a piña colada with a shitload of rum in it.

I didn't drink again until I was about fifteen, so I was quite a late starter. We went to the rec and we were sitting on the swings while people played rave music on their phones (we were dead cool).

My friend had kept an open bottle of Lambrini underneath her bed for two weeks and it tasted so bad we tried to dilute it with blueberry Panda Pops. She also had a quarter litre of cheap vodka so we added that too and I think I got alcohol poisoning. I vommed everywhere and had the proper shakes.

When I got home my parents could totally tell. I hate the smell of Chinese food so my dad purposely ordered one for himself so I'd learn my lesson. It bloody worked because I didn't drink again until I went to sixth-form college.

The first pub we ever managed to get into was when I was

only fifteen, and the lads would get a pint in and we'd drink Coke and play pool. God knows how I got in because I looked so young and I still get asked for ID now.*

My friends and I talk about really random stuff when we're together and sometimes that pre-going-out loud, shouty hour is my favourite part of the night. We're weird friends in a way, but I feel like you know you've got a great set of mates when you can talk about really strange stuff and no one questions it. There's a real variety relationship-wise and some of my friends are engaged or married, while others have been single for years. One of my mates has got twin babies so she hardly ever comes out, but when she does it makes me feel dead guilty about how ridiculous I am. She's trying to bring up two small children and the rest of us are talking about whether pouring vodka into our eyeballs would get us drunk quicker.

Sometimes when we're chatting I'll say, 'This is why we're single,' because some of the things we discuss are ludicrous and any lad who was listening would think we were unhinged.

Me single mates all think I'm weird cos I'm not always texting with a lad. Anytime we're out, they'll all be on their phones. But I think people have lowered their basic standards for what's classed as an interesting conversation. They'll get a message saying, 'What R U Up 2?' and they show you it and they're like, 'He's dead funny and flirty.' I can't be bothered

---

* There used to be so much strategy about getting served in pubs. All the lads would be like 'go in jangling some keys and complaining about traffic and your job and that. That'll make you sound old enough.' All the girls just wore a push-up bras.

with all those constant updates. It's hard dating now, even compared to three years ago. Social media has just gone mental.

Tinder

I don't get Tinder. Some men have a photo of them getting married as their Tinder photo. I'm sometimes sitting next to my mate and a picture of a penis flashes up and I'm like, 'What was that?!' And she's like, 'Oh, we've been messaging.' One minute you're messaging and it's all, 'How was your day?' and then the next minute there's a picture of a penis. I block them straight away but I have a mate who's like, 'Give him a chance.' I'm like delete, block, done.

It's not exactly the most romantic story for the grandkids, is it? 'I met your granddad on a dating website and then he showed me a photograph of his penis and I knew he was the one.'

I've always been a bit sceptical about dating apps, but I put myself on Tinder a while ago because everyone was raving about it. I was sat at home ready to look through loads of profiles, but after I swiped right on three lads thinking they were probably knobheads it said, 'You've run out of people in your area.' I set my distance to within forty kilometres! How can there only be three people to reject within forty kilometres? That right there is why I'm going to be alone for ever.

There's also not much mystery when you meet someone online because on some sites you already know if they want to settle down or not, if they've got kids, what they do . . . What have you got to find out on a first date? Where's that excitement? Although having said that, some people will say they're not looking for a relationship – code for just wanting sex – but how do they know? They could meet the love of their life.

Loads of my friends are on Plenty of Fish, but I would honestly rather just meet someone in real life. It's really shallow judging someone simply on a photo and you're basically saying to them, 'I don't like the look of you and can't be bothered to give you the time of day.' They could be the nicest person in the world, but if they don't look nice in their photo, they're fucked.

I also get guys asking if I'm 'her off *Gogglebox*' and I deny it and pretend someone's set up a fake profile in my name. I know, it's twatty. Someone once tweeted and said, 'I've just seen Scarlett Moffatt on Tinder', and I got really defensive and said it wasn't me. I don't know why I lied; I was just embarrassed.

One of my mates saw this guy she liked on Plenty of Fish and she kept showing us his picture. I knew I recognized him from somewhere so we did some digging via Facebook, and it turned out that the reason I knew him is because he'd been in the papers the week before. It was a big news story because he'd set light to all the pot pouri in his ex-girlfriend's house. Her house may have smelt lovely when she walked in, though.

I don't send rude Snapchats either. On Snapchat I mostly send photos of dogs and stupid selfies where I'm pulling faces.

And I've never done the whole 'Netflix and chill' thing. Well, I went round to my mate's house to watch a film with him and told my friends, and they just kept raising their eyebrows and I had to be like, 'No, I'm actually watching Netflix.' I reckon the reason it's a thing now is that there are no films you want to watch on there, so you end up making your own entertainment. I can't decide whether Netflix will be dead happy with the saying or not.

Group roles

We've all kind of got different roles in my friendship group. My mates may disagree, but I think Sam and I are the funny ones. We're like the Ant and Dec of the group. Sometimes we'll have a conversation between us for fifteen minutes and no one else will speak during that time because they're too busy listening to us two talking shit.

Sarah is like the mam of the group, so she's the one who always makes sure everyone is all right and she's quite sensible. She's still dead funny but she keeps us in check and if it wasn't for her I'd probably be dead or in prison. At the end of the night, when someone is suggesting we go on to an awful club, she'll be the one to rein us in. I also behave myself a lot more when she's around, which is a very good thing.

Kelly's the really bad influence. Say it gets to 1 a.m. and someone says, 'Shall we have one more and head off?' she'll be like, 'Or we could do this . . .' and I'll end up getting in at 10 a.m. She always knows someone who's having a house party somewhere, and we're not even sure how she knows these people let alone how she knows they're having a party.

There's this girl I know whose sole purpose of going on a night out is to meet a lad. She'll be really keen to go to a certain bar and when we get there we'll spot a boy she likes. I don't know why she tries to be sneaky about it because we all know what she's up to, but we play dumb because it adds to the fun of it.

My friend Hannah is really shy when she's sober, but as soon as she's drunk she turns into a proper crazy woman. It's like she's been possessed by the spirit of a drunken lunatic and she'll be dancing like a nutter and talking to anyone and everyone.

I tend to find that it's my friends who have got kids who are the ones who will get most wasted on a night out. It's like, in their head, they've only got one night every few months to really enjoy themselves, so they're properly unleashed. Thankfully they don't spend all night talking about their kids. Can you imagine how boring that would be? I mean, I like some kids, but I don't want to bloody chat about them.

Mad shit

This is the part of the night where we'll just talk about whatever's in our head. Quite often we'll just say the name of a celebrity or something that's in the news and then everyone will start weighing in with their opinion. I'm going to choose a small selection of the things we've talked about recently.

Justin Bieber

What can you say about the Bieber? He's got more followers than the population of the UK. He looks like Ellen DeGeneres. He's twenty-two and he's a multi-millionaire. Of course he's surrounded by supermodels and fast cars. Who wouldn't be?

At twenty-two any millionaire celeb would park on the street because they can afford the parking fine.

But he could get better hair.

Someone told me he just wears his Calvin Klein pants once and then throws them away. I can believe that. I bet he doesn't even get them out the box. His assistant has to open the boxes at the beginning of the week and lay his week's pants out for him. That's like part of their job description: Pant Opener.

And I reckon he wears more than one pair a day on average. And Calvin Klein are like £35 per pair of pants. So let's say ten pairs a week, cos some days he doesn't change his pants. That's £350 a week, or £18k a year.

At some point in the future there'll be oil that's mainly made from Bieber pants. I bet that's like the most premium oil ever.

If I was him, I'd sell them on eBay. I might pitch that as a business. Bieberpants.com. 'Hello Dragons, I am looking for £400,000 for a 1.5 per cent stake in my company, Bieberpants. com.'

But he does have shit hair. It's swings and roundabouts really. Maybe he'd rather have less followers and nice hair.

Beyoncé

Everyone absolutely bops her and I don't understand why. Mainly Beyoncé wiggles her arse about, doesn't she, and it is a very impressive arse. It feels like that will never stop being a way to be famous. I like a lot of her music, but people talk as if she's changing the world. Mainly, though, I'm sick of everyone tagging Jay-Z and Beyoncé in photos and hashtagging them #relationshipgoals. They'll be there cuddling and people start saying they want a relationship like Jay-Z and Beyoncé. To be fair, I reckon some of the people saying that have probably had their sister beat their boyfriend up in a lift. Achievable goals and all that.

Maybe if you stopped hashtagging on your phone and actually talked to a human being you'd have a relationship.

Bad Girls

I feel like I spent most of my young teen life watching *Bad Girls*. It's that ITV show where they're in prison. It was amazing. I'm not sure if I should have watched it – it was pretty racy for then. The first time I ever saw a girl kiss a girl was in that t.A.T.u video and then suddenly the video was everywhere. They were, like, young Russian girls and you weren't sure how much they were into it, or whether there was something else going on. 'OK, if we kiss now, we can see family?' It was a catchy song, though. And then they just disappeared. Maybe they're in the same place as the Cheeky Girls?

Also, I reckon that's where Will.i.am got his idea for spelling his name like that.

Jamie Oliver

I can rag on Jamie Oliver all day. I don't know why he exists. He saps the fun out of everything. A sugar tax?! He still serves sugary drinks at his restaurants, doesn't he? He said, 'Oh, I've made them more expensive,' but don't serve them at all if you feel that strongly. I swear, his wife deserves a medal the size of a dustbin lid. I don't know how she copes. I remember the Naked Chef back in the day when he was playing drums and riding a moped. My sister will never know the joy of chocolate cake in pink custard, because he's got rid of it. No potato smiley faces. Why would you do that to kids?

Everyone I know basically ate chips, turkey drummers and beans every meal. And we turned out all right. Sometimes it would be green custard and then everyone would be in such a good mood for the rest of the day. You used to get mashed potato in an ice-cream scoop. They have a pasta bar at my little sister's school. They don't need a pasta bar, they're nine. There's plenty of time for pasta bars. Everyone talks about kids growing up too fast because of the internet and music videos, but no one's talking about pasta bars. Let kids be kids!

I watched his annual Christmas programme and his advice was basically to cook the entire meal in goose fat. And now he's all worried about sugar? I reckon it's just a fashion thing, isn't it? Even Nigella has gone healthy because everyone else has.

His fifteen-minute-meals thing – it was basically just showing off. 'Look how quickly I can do my job.' It's like me showing off how quickly I can change the printer cartridge or something. It's bad enough when you try and make something off the TV and it doesn't look like it should, now you just have one more thing to worry about: that you haven't made it quickly enough. My mates always say that he does loads of good with the Fifteen restaurant and stuff, but that doesn't make up for the pasta bars in schools.

Big Brother

The first few series of *Big Brother* were amazing. I can still remember those early people. There was Craig the builder. And that fellah that lied and said he was SAS and then he couldn't get over the assault course. Nasty Nick. And Nicky Graham. I could relate to her because I went through a phase when I only drank bottled water. And she only drank bottled water, so I felt like I knew where she was coming from. See I'm not the only one. That blonde Kate who's a DJ. Now it's on Channel Five, I don't even know when it's on most of the time.

Superheroes

Superman looks exactly the same when he puts his glasses on and combs his hair and everyone acts like it's someone else. I don't buy it. Batman has a proper disguise. I can't remember who said it, but it's true, Superman isn't brave. It's not brave to fight people if you know they can't hurt you.

I don't understand why female superheroes aren't dressed a bit more practically. It's all leather trousers and low-cut tops. It basically implies that the only reason Scarlett Johansson's character is in *Avengers* is that she's on the pull.

Jeremy Clarkson

He's so overrated. He's a posh knobhead. He thinks he's so big he can do what he wants. Everyone's always like, 'He's old school,' and I'm like, 'My granddad's old school, but he never thumped an employee.' How old is this school, like Vikings

Upside down with me dad. I think I've probably spent my whole life trying to find something as fun as this.

Chillaxing. I clearly haven't learnt to sit forward on the sofa yet.

Looking good. (Yes, I think those are knickers in the background.)

In me checked
dress, looking
like butter
wouldn't melt.

Hair up and ready to do
a human sacrifice on my
little cousin.

*Gogglebox
Scarlett in
topless shocker!*

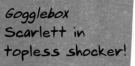

Try telling me this hat isn't awesome. You can't. It is.

With me mam. I'm sorry, I know you might think you're the best dancer, but it's actually me and I have the certificate to prove it.

The brows, the brows!

Double-strawing it.

A selection of 'strong looks', including braids!

Me touching some sort of squealing fish.

Just about to go and do my old-fogie dancing.

I loved that fur coat at the time. *sigh*

Me with a bloody massive ring on me finger.

Eighteen-years-old and shy and retiring.

Strictly Scarlett.

Freshers Week.

The girls: (clockwise from top left)
me, Sarah, Hannah, Billie, Sam and Kellie.

I was so
much more
into the
mouse ears
than my
sister, Ava.

On the sofa for Gogglebox with me mam and dad.

or something? He's like Prince Philip: he just wanders in and insults whole countries. It's not funny, man, it's rude.

And I bet he refers to himself at The Clarkson. 'Hey, bar wench, The Clarkson needs another pint of beer.' What does he spend his money on? Dad jeans and leather jackets and a gentle perm.

I don't get *Top Gear*. It's like a fetish. How can you like cars that much? At least with property shows there's a sense of real people in the houses and a bit of a story, like Susan is doing up her teenage daughter's bedroom or something. But if they did property shows like *Top Gear* they'd be all 'we test the ten biggest lounges in the UK' and then there'd just be all these middle-aged men competitively sitting on the sofa, secretly hating each other and bullying each other and calling it banter. I hate the studio audience in *Top Gear*. They always put all the women up front. If someone got me tickets to go and watch *Top Gear* being filmed, I'd never talk to them again.

The new *Top Gear* is with Chris Evans, isn't it? They should actually show normal people using cars. Instead it's always just been knobheads driving around. My dad doesn't like it and I'm really glad. I'd hate it if he was one of those Clarkson dads.

The Da Vinci Code

I didn't read the book but I watched the film and I don't understand why Da Vinci didn't just write what was going on on the back of the painting straight out. 'Jesus = Daddy.' Instead of having a statue pointing to a thing in Latin that's an anagram. It was basically just all the famous people in art that normal people have heard of. Leonardo da Vinci, Shakespeare, yep, all of them, it's all the same.

It's like, why do aliens bother blowing up the Taj Mahal and the White House and the Eiffel Tower in films? If they're powerful enough to destroy the planet, why would they bother with landmarks? They'd be blowing up the big cities in China where most people are, not Big Ben. It'd be like you going to pour water on an ants' nest and working out which bit you think is the important bit.

The ten most embarrassing things celebrities have ever said

1) When Christina Aguilera was asking where the Cannes film festival was being held . . .
Speechless.

2) Kanye West: 'I'm like a vessel, and God has chosen me to be the voice and the connector.'
Somehow I don't think God would have chosen an egotistical, miserable man who raps about money and bitches and whose right-hand woman leaked her own sex tape. He's no Moses, is he?

3) Justin Bieber on Anne Frank: 'Hopefully she would have been a Belieber.'
Personally I think that listening to auto-tuned pop music would have been the last thing on her mind.

4) In 2007 Miss Teen South Carolina was asked, 'Polls have shown a fifth of Americans can't locate the US on a world map. Why do you think this is?' Her reply? 'They are unable to do so because, uh, some, uh, people out there in our nation don't have maps and, uh, I believe that our education like such as in South Africa and, uh, the Iraq, everywhere like such as, and, I believe that they should help.'

Sorry?

5) Brooke Shields' famous anti-smoking speech: 'Smoking kills. If you're killed, you've lost a very important part of your life.'

Thanks for clearing that up.

6) Arnold Schwarzenegger's insistence that 'gay marriage should be between a man and a woman.'

He's clever, that one.

7) The wisdom of Jaden Smith: 'How can mirrors be real if our eyes aren't real?'

What are they? Pretend ones?

8) David Beckham when his eldest son was born: 'I want Brooklyn to be christened, but don't know into what religion yet.'

He may be beautiful, but he's definitely missing some brains.

9) Ivana Trump on writing novels: 'Fiction writing is great. You can make up almost anything.'

Sigh.

10) Joey Essex when asked if he knew why we celebrated Guy Fawkes Night: 'No, not really. He died on the cross or something, on a bonfire, didn't he?'
No, Joey. He didn't.

Harry Potter

I love *Harry Potter*. My theory is that you're either a *Harry Potter* or a *Lord of the Rings* person. I read the books and I remember thinking Daniel Radcliffe looks exactly like I had imagined him in my head. I love Emma Watson too. I'm totally a *Harry Potter* fan. Hermione was better at magic than the boys and she made it OK to have frizzy hair. She was my role model.

I used to love Roald Dahl too. *The Witches* was terrifying. You never got told how the nan lost her thumb, just that it was something to do with the head witch. And there was the girl that got trapped in the painting and she got older and older, and sometimes she'd be by the gate, and sometimes she'd be out feeding the chickens and that, until one day she died. I mean, people save up their entire lives to be able to retire to a house in the country with some chickens. And I used to think that maybe all the mice that you see are really kids who've been changed into mice.

Doppelgängers

I reckon we've all got one. A little while ago I met my actual doppelgänger. People kept calling me Catherine when I was out, and I was confused at first. And then we bumped into each other and I was all, 'Is your name Catherine?' and she knew I was Scarlett because people had kept calling us the wrong name when we'd gone out.

Hoovers

Me two-year-old cousin is obsessed with hoovers. There was this Dyson advert on the telly and whenever it came on he would just shout, 'hoov, hoov, hoov!' We had to rewind it and keep showing it to him or he'd get really upset. And round where my auntie lives, someone had left a hoover in the back alley for the council to take away and he kept going, 'I wanna touch it.' And she kept saying, 'You can't touch it.' He was leaning right out of his pushchair as he went past. She had to do a detour every day on the way to nursery so he could look at it. He was stretching out of the pram to touch it. He's literally obsessed. He'll get me dad and be like, 'Uncy Mark, Uncy Mark, hoove.' And me dad has to get the hoover out and he'll move it back and forth over the same bit of carpet. He's interested in any vacuum cleaner but Dysons are his favourite.* There's a place on the corner that does them and sometimes me mam will take him there as a treat.

Bradley Cooper

He is a conventionally good-looking man, isn't he?

---

* Full disclosure: if Mr Dyson is reading this, a hoover would be completely appreciated. Or if you do tours of the factory or anything.

Calpol

It's just the most delicious thing. I reckon you could sell cocktails mixed with Calpol in bars and people would go mad for
it. But the pink one, with the sugar in it, not that sugar-free
nonsense.

Guantanamo Bay

We were talking about this because the last British person that
was there had just been released. But I remember when I was
a kid everyone was talking about it when it was set up and I
didn't really understand what it was but I thought it sounded
like a magical place, like a holiday camp or something, with
free drinks and a swimming pool. It feels like the sort of
name people would show off about going to: 'Well, we're off
to Guantanamo Bay this summer.' And then you find out
what it is and it's not at all fun, is it? I just think it's a very
misleading name. 'What are you going to do in Guantanamo
Bay?' 'Ah, we'll probably do some waterboarding.' It still
sounds inappropriately fun!

Differences between north and south

It does piss me off that whenever there's a news story about
the north-east, they go and film some fat people in tracksuits
kind of hobbling up and down. They have those people down
south too. And what they never say is that we have a canny
time up here. Yes, we may only live till we're sixty-seven, but
there's plenty of booze and laughs in the meantime. And we

don't give a shit. Down south, all they do is walk past each other and moan about the Tube.

Having said that, I saw a toaster down south the other day that had two dials on it. I've never seen a two-dial toaster up north. Travel definitely broadens the mind.

Jennifer Lawrence

I love her. When she fell over, she did it so sweetly. It's amazing that she's basically the biggest star in the world and she comes across so normal. There's that amazing footage of her getting properly excited cos Jack Nicholson was chatting her up at the Oscars.

Ellen

I'm addicted to watching clips of her on the internet. She's always talking about happy things. That's what I like about America, they're much more likely to have uplifting stuff on. And I think I maybe like her cos she looks like Justin Bieber.

Ariana Grande

She's another one of those used-to-be Disney girls who went all sexy and grown-up. I swear, they want to look at that Disney TV thing. She does an amazing Celine Dion impression too. I saw her doing it on Jimmy Fallon and it was brilliant.

Selena Gomez

I know her mainly as Justin Bieber's ex. I think it's a bit weird that everyone's obsessed with these people we've all seen as children and now they're all writhing around in leather trousers and no top and that.

We live in such a weird world that you can basically make a living from the size of your boobs. When it's all *Mad Max* and people are digging back through the sand and trying to work out what happened, and there's no electricity so they have to work out what it was like in the past just from newspapers and they'll have the *Daily Star* and the *Sun* to go on, there'll just be all these stories about what people were saying on Twitter and they'll probably think Twitter was the name of a god or something.

September 11th

I remember getting in from school and my dad saying, 'You need to watch this because it's history,' and I didn't think it was real because it was so much like a film. And then the next day at school the teachers had the televisions on, and that's all we were doing, just watching. It's shaped everything, hasn't it? It's mad to think that, in fifty years, kids will be learning about it in history and we lived through it.

Taylor Swift

She appears to be mainly built of elbows. She's all joints, man.

Jeremy Kyle

I saw an episode of *Jeremy Kyle* the other day and it blew my mind. The title was: 'I'm both the step-grandfather and the father of a baby girl.' He was this girl's stepdad and then he got together with the daughter and they had a baby. Seventy-five million years and that's what we've evolved into. Jesus, no wonder monkeys look sad when you see them in the zoo.

Zoos

While we're on the subject of animals, I have to say that I do not like zoos. In a hundred years' time I think we'll look back and wonder why the hell we caged these majestic animals. I don't even like going to aquariums. The first time I went to Blackpool Tower when I was about eight, I cried because they kept a giant turtle in a tank. It had sad eyes and it kept bouncing off the sides, and even thinking about it now upsets me. I don't mind it when animals are in captivity because they may become extinct if we don't help them, but anything else is wrong.

It's so horrible when you see monkeys pacing up and down because they've lost the plot. And if a monkey bit someone's hand off, they'd put it down. I'm not being funny, but if I was a monkey I'd do the same.

Ava keeps saying she wants to go to a zoo but I keep explaining why they're not good. I've never been to one and I don't want to. I'm not about to go and protest outside one with a giant placard, dressed as a gorilla, but equally I don't embrace them.

Criminals

I hate crime, full stop. I hate people doing bad things to each other. Why would you? All crimes are crimes, but I feel like only people who commit petty crimes should have access to TVs and PlayStations in prison. People who commit much more serious crimes should have some *actual* punishment, not be allowed to watch *Corrie* of an evening. Why should people who have done bad things have privileges that some people who haven't committed crimes can't afford?

I do love watching *Crimewatch*, though. Is that bad? I always hope I'm going to see someone I know on it.

A friend of mine is an occupational therapist and she works with criminals, and she can't read any of the cases because she'd rather not know what they've done unless they tell her. She said one of them had done something awful but he was really good-looking and it freaked her out that if he'd come up to her in a bar she probably would have fancied him.

When I was at university I was in the hockey society and we had some mint nights out. There was a fancy dress party one evening and because we were in the first year we had to go dressed as robbers, while the girls in the years above went as cops. My mates and I were dressed up in striped jumpers with swag bags drinking cocktails and loving life.

When Sarah and I got home drunk our front door was on the latch. We could hear people in the house and we thought it was just our flatmates Jess and Zoe. I peered into Jess's room and it looked as messy as it always did but all of her drawers were pulled out and something didn't seem right. All of a sudden Sarah and I clicked on to the fact we'd been burgled and I started screaming.

When we eventually went into the house everything was everywhere. The robbers had thrown a paving slab through the double-glazing to get in and had stolen a load of stuff. They took tons of our expensive things, like laptops, but they also took more personal stuff, like photos, which freaked me out.

I phoned the police and when they turned up Sarah and I were standing in the street still dressed as robbers. I was crying but the police thought we were taking the piss and told us that prank calls are an arrestable offence! How unlucky were we to get burgled when we were dressed as robbers?

None of us wanted to stay in the house that night so Sarah's mam drove in the middle of the night to pick us up. When she arrived she looked around the house and she was horrified by the mess the robbers had made in my room. The thing is, the only thing they'd taken from it was my computer. They hadn't touched the rest; it looked exactly the same before they broke in. That floor-drobe was all my doing.

Carrier bags

The whole carrier-bag thing winds me up. I pay tax – give me a bag, man! I hate it when you go into a shop and they ask you if you want a bag when you've got twenty things. Of course I do. I'm not an octopus.

I don't want to have to carry a load of plastic bags around with me all the time. We live across the road from Asda and sometimes I'll take the trolley home with me and unpack my

shopping, and then wheel the trolley back because I refuse to pay 15 pence for three bags. It's the principal. It did make me laugh the other day when there was a story in the paper about how you can get around the charge, and their tip was 'bring your own plastic bags', as if that was somehow cheating the system. That's exactly the point of it!

David Cameron

No one ever really likes the prime minister, but he's not to blame for everything.

The whole pig thing was very unfortunate for him, wasn't it? He's never going to be able to eat a sausage sandwich in public again, is he? Everyone does crazy things at uni and even if he did put his bits in a pig's mouth, so what? Although I did find it funny the next day when loads of people were putting up fake labels for pork pies and sausage rolls on Twitter with 'David Cameron's penis' listed as one of the ingredients.

I feel a bit sorry for him. He's aged so much in the last five years. He looked quite young and buff and he had loads of hair back in the day, but he's aged about thirty years in no time. It's all those worries. Although, I mean, if we're comparing him to Gordon Brown or Jeremy Corbyn, he's quite fit really. Corbyn looks more like the next Dr Who than the next fucking prime minister to me. Cameron's no Hugh Grant in *Love Actually* but he's the best of a bad bunch.

Actually, I hate Hugh Grant. He basically made a whole generation of men think they just had to blink and stutter and talk quietly and it was sexy. And have floppy hair. He basically invented the *Made in Chelsea* boys. For that he deserves to be punished.

The NHS

When I watch programmes like *One Born Every Minute* and *24 Hours in A&E* I just think the NHS is amazing and we're so lucky to have it in this country. Even people who don't have money can get cared for and you can't say that about many places in the world. In some countries people can't actually afford to be well, which seems so crazy.

Me dad had vertigo once when he and me mam were on holiday in Spain and when they went to the Spanish hospital people were piled up in corridors and the queues were crazy. I know the food's a bit shit in our hospitals and they can smell a bit pissy, but they're saving people's lives, so you can't really moan.

We're lucky to have such good doctors too. I always think when I go to the doctor's that I'll get a fit one, but I never have. Gutted. It's funny how doctors always ask if you're OK. No, I'm at the doctor's, of course I'm bloody not. I don't like the fact they know everything about you too. I mean, *everything*. That scares me. What if I do fancy a doctor sometime and he's read all me notes about the time I had a dodgy tummy? He's hardly going to fancy me then, is he? It must be weird if you're married to a gynaecologist. They're at work all day and then they get home and the last thing they probably want to look at is another one. It'd be a right busman's holiday.

I'm a proper drama queen when it comes to being ill. Every time I have a really bad hangover I google me symptoms and think I'm dying. Or I'll get a headache behind one eye and convince myself I've got a brain tumour. Rabies, scabies and jelly babies, that's me. I've always got something. Don't ever google your symptoms when you're feeling shit, because there are only ever two outcomes – you're either dying or you're pregnant. I'm one of those people the doctors must dread because I've already diagnosed meself.

Brothels

Carrying on with the political theme, let's talk about brothels. One of my favourite places in the world to go is Amsterdam. It's beautiful and I also find it hilarious. It's so bizarre that people go to London to see the Christmas windows, but when you go to Amsterdam you go and have a look at all the women in the windows. You can always see men coming out of brothels looking dead sheepish and they scuttle off down the street.

I think if it were to make the women safer, brothels should be legalized. But then again, I'm not sure it would be good to promote that kind of thing. What would the advert look like in the paper? And what would you call the place? Open all hours? I find it weird that there's a need for it. There's plenty to see on the internet, isn't there? I've never really understood it, but I guess I'm not a man . . .

Pigeons

If any of you read my tweets, you'll know I'm obsessed with baby pigeons. I'd always wondered why you never see them and now I know. I looked them up the other day and they're bloody ugly. I reckon they hide away until they get older because they're so horrible looking. Seriously, google them.

Pigeons are evil and they nick your chips up north. I'm not a fan. But I saw some kids kicking one once and I felt dead sad for it. I told my dad about it and he said you're allowed to kick them because they're vermin. I'm not sure that's true. And even if it is, I don't think that's OK. They may be ugly chip nickers but they don't deserve violence.

Badgers

I use badgers in every phrase going. I say 'crazy as a badger', 'cock-eyed as a badger', 'mad as a badger' . . . I don't know why but they're quite a vital part of my diction.

The badger cull is horrible. And they are vicious little things, but you still can't go around shooting badgers. Who do people think they are? Badgers can't defend themselves from guns. Leave the badgers alone.

Were badgers around on earth before humans? I reckon they probably were, so they've got more right to be here than we have. Even if they weren't, you can't just go into badgers' homes and start shooting around, can you? What's wrong with the world? I'm going to start a petition. Even if just a few people from my Twitter sign up for it, we can help them.

Weddings

We'll almost always have someone in our extended circle who's getting married, so it's a constant topic of conversation.

I love weddings, and my best mate Sarah is getting married soon and I'm dead excited. I'm always the bridesmaid.

There's something magical about a wedding. I love the fact that someone is saying, 'I like you that much that I want to spend the rest of my life with you.'

I also love the fact that something normally kicks off because I enjoy a drama. I love all the wedding food and all the cheesy songs and I'm always the first one on the dance floor and the last one off. I properly go for it and by the end I'm sweating like a fat man at a buffet.

For some reason I become a sign language expert when I'm dancing at weddings and I act out all the songs. If a deaf person was watching me, they would totally know what song I was dancing to. In fact, that should be a quiz on the telly.*

Ed Sheeran

One thing I'm a bit over is every wedding I go to at the moment having a song by Ed Sheeran. All his songs sound the same and I'm sick of hearing them. I've been to, like, five, where they've played the same song and it just makes me feel sad. Me mam and dad's generation had Marvin Gaye and I've got Ed Sheeran. Although actually, they told me the other day they mainly had 'Lady in Red' in their day, so maybe that's not much better.

Although I do really love the fact Ed Sheeran looks like he's wandered on stage through the wrong door. Like he's in

---

* Channel Four, if you're reading, it could be called 'Scarlett Dances the Hits'.

on work experience or something. America has Justin Bieber, who's like something made in a lab by teenage girls. And we've got someone who looks like he sits out on the grass at sixth-form college with a guitar. He looks like he's just about to tell you about his gap year and that.

Also, loads of his songs feel like they're from someone doing a play in GCSE drama. *I'm gonna do a song about drugs and bullying and peer pressure.* I did really like that video where he was a muppet, though. Anyone who's got a puppet of themselves as a muppet is all right in my book.

Marriage

I do think about getting married, and of course more than ever when I go to a wedding. I feel like Disney has given me unrealistic expectations of marriage. I used to want a handsome prince charming, but then I started to like all the evil ones like Gaston. If you had to choose between the Beast in *Beauty and the Beast* when he's a monster or when he's that wussy prince, I'd choose the Beast. Having said that, Ava said the other day, 'Why does Belle fancy a dog?' which is a fair point.

I try to drum it into my little sister that she doesn't need a prince. I'm so glad Disney made *Frozen* because that's about the sisters and there's no man coming along to make sure everything is OK. In all the old ones the heroines were saved by lads, but that's so old-fashioned. Disney needs to make some more modern films where women save the day.

Proposals

I've always said to me mam that if someone proposes to me on my birthday, Christmas, New Year or Valentine's Day, I'll say no because no thought would've gone into it. I know I'm too picky but I want someone to put a proper effort in and surprise me. But it doesn't have to be a really grand gesture.

I feel like, all of a sudden, engagements have to be this massive thing and really elaborate, and half the time I think they only do it so they can put it on social media. There's all those videos of people who've learnt dances and miming along to songs and stuff – they're whole productions.

My friend Sarah's fiancé proposed to her on Christmas Day by putting a ring on a sausage. That's funny, but she was saying, 'I can't really put that on Facebook.' But who cares? It's a private moment for you two. It's no one else's business. And if I see one more status update saying, 'He put a ring on it', I'll fucking scream.

I have *kind of* been planning my wedding since I was young but I haven't worked out the finer details because it depends who I end up with. If I marry someone that hasn't got a lot of money, I'll get married in a registry office and then go to the pub. If I marry someone rich, I want to arrive at the venue on a unicorn (when I say venue, I mean castle).

Me mam says I've got really tacky wedding taste but I think Jordan's marriage to Peter Andre was amazing. I loved it. I want mine to be like that. I want a glass carriage. Why the fuck wouldn't you? I'd also like a Willy Wonka theme. I'd have all the centrepieces as sweets and I'd have Munchkins as waiters. I love Johnny Depp, so I could marry him. Or if he's not

free to be my husband, then the groom can dress up as him. But when he was in *Edward Scissorhands*, not when he looks like a wino pirate.

One of the main reasons I want a wedding is so I can get loads of presents. I want people to buy me blenders and shit. I want a NutriBullet and that's a great way to get one. In fact, I reckon I might extend my *Ocean's Eleven* stunt so that I get all the wedding presents with a fake wedding.

I don't really like it when people ask for money for their wedding gift. I think it's a bit rude. I do give it to them but I'm a bit resentful about it, like. I know people don't want toasters any more but I feel weird about handing over cash or putting money into people's bank accounts. It feels like in *The Office* when Dawn's boyfriend says he just tells her to take the money out of his wallet and buy her own birthday present. We might as well just not get each other anything as it all evens out. If I don't get married, I'm invoicing all the people I've bought wedding presents for to get the money back.

Some days I get really excited about the prospect of getting married, and other days I think, *I'm a strong, independent woman* and I can't picture myself sitting at home with two kids day after day. I like to think I'll meet someone who's adventurous that I could go travelling with and stuff. He'll probably have to be a millionaire. Is that shallow?

Tess Daly

I don't get her. She has no enthusiasm in her voice, she just sucks the excitement out of everything. She's like an eight-year-old boy's idea of how to draw of a pretty lady. 'She'd be a blonde lady with boobies and a face.' I love Claudia Winkleman and I feel like Tesss's always patronizing to her. I reckon she treats Claudia like a slightly slow old man, the ghost of Brucey in between them. Claudia gets a load of stick about her make-up and I don't understand it. She looks great. And I thought what she did after her daughter's Halloween costume caught fire was amazing. It was just the most terrifying thing and she was able to talk about it to make sure other people knew what could happen.

Katie Hopkins

She only wants to be controversial. Something happens and you're just waiting for her to say something mean about it. I know I shouldn't give her the attention, but it makes me angry. She was actually OK on *Big Brother*. My theory is that she didn't have the time for her team to come up with shocking opinions, so she was just normal. She seems to say something controversial like clockwork. There's a disaster or something and all these kittens die in a fire in an orphanage and everyone's saying how awful it is and she's like, 'They were foreign kittens, the orphanage shouldn't have been open anyway and the fire was started by an immigrant.'

I loved it when she was on *Good Morning* doing a thing about how it was tacky for people to name their children after places in the world, like Paris and Brooklyn. And Holly Willoughby laid the smackdown on her and pointed out her daughter is called India. Surely if you're going on TV knowing you're talking about that subject, you'd think that one through?

I can't be the only one that's bored by her. The thing is, she reads all of her press, so I wouldn't be surprised if she finds out about this and slags me off. I wonder what she'll say. Probably something about my appearance cos she likes doing that, or maybe she'll imply I'm thick. I'll get in first. Yes, I know I look like an oompa loompa. I'm genuinely excited now to see what happens.

Caitlyn Jenner

I think what she's done is amazing and it's helping make the subject much more visible. But there's a little bit of me that feels the way it's happened in her life is not how most people could ever approach things. She's got all this amazing support and she basically picked what she wanted to look like out of a catalogue and then had the money to buy it.

There was that story a while back when she auditioned famous transgender people to be her friends on her reality show. I'm a bit torn because on one level it's good but, like all of that stuff, it's not all real. It's great that Eddie Redmayne is in that film about the first person who ever had a transgender operation. There are some things I'd be up for being the first to do, but that's something I'd want to know they'd done a few times before.

Russell Brand

I love him. I think he gets a hard time. But I do reckon the sexaholic thing is a bit of a cop-out – he's just a player, there's no need to make a medical thing out of it. Stop it, keep it in your trousers. But when I'm listening to him I feel like I'm listening to a poem. He makes me want to go and google words. He's like the opposite of Jeremy Clarkson. He uses words in a lovely way. He does look a bit grubby, though. My mate described him as being essentially handsome but a bit grubby. I'm not sure me dad would be happy if I brought him home. Having said that, it was ridiculous all that stuff about Manuel from *Fawlty Towers'* granddaughter. It wasn't the nicest thing in the world to do but it's not the worst thing anyone has ever done.

Robbie Williams

I only really knew him on his own. I don't remember Take That first time around. People of me mam's generation think of Take That as hot young men doing somersaults on the beach. I remember them as some old men on a roof in Marks & Spencer coats. Gary Barlow is a man so boring that the most exciting thing he ever did involved dodgy tax planning.

That video where Robbie Williams is singing his own songs at his wife as she's giving birth . . . I tell you, if that'd been me, I'd have bashed him round the head with the gas and air canister.

I just remember that 'Rock DJ' song's video getting banned where Robbie got his skin peeled off. Me mam let me stay up late to watch it. I had a really early bedtime all the way through school. I'm pretty sure I had like a 9 p.m. bedtime officially till after A Levels. So my whole teenage years were spent with me pretending to be interested in things that were on a little bit later than my bedtime. And if you wanted to take the day off the next day, you'd have to plant the seed the day before. You'd fuss about with your tea, so they'd think you were really ill. I remember putting my hand near the fire and then putting it on my head and getting my mam to feel how hot my forehead was. I'd spend the whole of Sunday pretending to be ill so I could have Monday off. I once sat so close to the fire to make my head feel hot that me eyebrows got singed. I think that's a real thing up north, the daughters getting a fuss made of them.

Me dad used to do so much for us when I was little. Whenever any of our animals died, because he's a welder, he would make a metal coffin. And when our goldfish died, he cut the finger off a velvet glove and buried him in that. That's why he'll do well in the zombie apocalypse cos of the welding. I was obsessed with my hamster, Lucky. If there's ever a name to tempt fate as a hamster, it's Lucky. I think my dad replaced him loads of times.

Steve Irwin

Do you remember him? The Australian guy who used to get all excited when he'd find a dangerous animal? I used to love Steve Irwin. He probably shouldn't have poked the animals so much, though.

The worst people I could be stuck in a bunker with

Karl Pilkington
If you're stuck in a bunker, you need to keep the positivity levels up, and Pilko would definitely spend the whole time moaning about being bored and how cramped it is.

Joe Pasquale
No offence, but his voice would irritate the life out of me, and his jokes are from the dawn of time.

The man from the Go Compare advert
This needs no explanation.

John McCririck
After seeing his lack of personal hygiene on *Celebrity Big Brother* (he wore the same underpants the entire time he was there) and his constant farting and nose picking, I'd end up vomiting.

Gillian McKeith
The woman's got a face like Alan Sugar's ball sack and takes great pleasure in analysing other people's shite and telling them how crap they are at life.

Katie Hopkins
I would end up having a full-on argument with her. No two ways about it.

Positive thinking

I think a lot of nonsense gets talked about positive thinking sometimes. Especially with all those things that get sent round on the internet of like a picture of a sunset and some words of wisdom. Sometimes you just want to have a good moan. My nanny thrives off of being negative. She'll come back from holiday and I'll be like, 'Oh, Nanny, how was your holiday?' and she'll go, 'It rained on the Wednesday, didn't it, Colin?' And me granddad's just sitting there nodding. 'Yeah, it did.'

You tell me if that doesn't sound fun.

Babies with loads of hair

I find it weird when babies are born with loads of hair, because that's been in someone's womb. It would freak me out if my baby came out and had more hair than me. I didn't get hair until I was three years old and I'm bald in all my baby photos, so maybe I'm just jealous of them?

The other thing I don't like is when babies are born with teeth. Hitler was born with teeth, which I think says it all.

Facebook fakers

One thing we regularly do is go on the internet and look at the people we know who are always posting photos so everyone can see what a good time they're having. There's always people you know like that. It's basically like they have the camera going with them in real time. The only problem is they spend so long trying to *look* like they are enjoying themselves they never really *do*.

I know this one girl who always looks like she's as miserable as hell on a night out, but as soon as someone starts taking photos she turns into the life and soul of the party. As soon as she's sees a flash go off she's practically doing jazz hands and wrapping herself around a lad she's met two minutes earlier. She posts pictures with captions like 'wild night' and 'crazy time' and I'm like, 'Wild night? You sat on a stool staring at your phone for most of the evening!'

I am very partial to a selfie meself but I think they also put a lot of pressure on people because it's all about how many likes you get. Everyone is guilty of deleting them if you don't get enough likes, and people base their self-worth on whether or not someone thinks they look nice in a photo.

If I had one wish, I would make it so that, for one day, whatever people looked like on the inside is how they looked on the outside. How amazing would that be? It would change so many people's perceptions. There are so many beautiful people who are arseholes, so it would be very telling. And the other way around: there are so many people that probably don't feel like they want to have photographs taken of them but who are so lovely.

Photographs

I used to really love my Polaroid camera when I was younger. I got in so much trouble with my dad for taking loads in one go because the film was so expensive. But I loved our normal camera too. One of the funniest things when you were a kid was going to get your photos developed and seeing how they came out. And there'd always be one of the floor or the celling because the camera had gone off by accident, or of your face from a weird angle. There was always one that looked like it was on fire. It's a feeling my sister's generation will never have. It's like with online shopping, where you can have something delivered four hours after you've placed the order. I've got friends with kids and whenever they're out you can hear them explaining to their kids that they can't have what they want as soon as they want it. We're living in a world where everyone can have their pudding first and it's making us all spoilt. You watch people editing photos again and again till they get them exactly right. If it looks like everyone has the perfect life with no effort, it makes people feel shit when their lives aren't like that. But no one's life is perfect without any effort, they're all pretending.

I've heard that some tribes believe that having your photograph taken takes away a piece of your soul. I reckon, having seen some of the people going for selfies in nightclubs, there's definitely something in that. I mean, I like taking a selfie with a pout as much as the next person, but some people take it to extremes, man. Their souls have definitely been stripped away.

Me mam and dad have all these albums of photos taken on special occasions and there are all these handwritten descriptions of what's happening, and it must have been so lovely to put together and they're so lovely to look at now. When was the last time you ever went back and looked at some digital photos? Photos used to mean something and now they don't and it's really sad.

It's the same way me sister can't understand that McDonald's used to be a treat, if you got a good school report or something. Or if your mam wanted to bribe you to come shopping and be good. I used to go to birthday parties at McDonald's. I told Ava that the other day and she looked at me like I was talking about going up the chimneys or something. She was one step away from patting me hand in sympathy.

Modern life

Even though I was bullied when I was a kid, I still think it's so much harder for girls growing up in the world today than it was when I was young. I worry for my little sister. It breaks my heart when I think about what she'll have to go through when she's a teenager. I honestly can't remember worrying one bit about what I looked like at primary school. Middle and secondary school, yes, but not when I was a kid.

I didn't compare myself to anyone and it didn't cross my mind that I was bigger or smaller than anyone else. If the dinner lady asked me if I wanted one scoop of mashed potato or two, it was always two, no question. I certainly wasn't watching my figure at the age of nine.

Ava says stuff to me about other kids' weight sometimes. She knows not to be awful about it and she would never say anything mean, but the fact she's aware of other people's size makes me so sad.

When I took her to school the other day I saw a girl of about ten with a full face of make-up on and I nearly started crying. She was covered in bronzer, mascara and loads of blusher and that scares me.

We all experiment with make-up and I remember going through a really awkward stage when I was twelve when I crimped my hair and wore really brightly coloured eye-shadows and a ton of lip gloss, but I didn't really know what I was doing.

Nowadays there are make-up ranges aimed specifically at young girls and I do think they're all growing up too fast. Some kids of twelve look about sixteen now, and their make-up looks like it's been done professionally. I honestly can't tell how old girls are any more because they dress and act so much older. I really hope it changes but I can't see that happening.

The fame game

The other thing that worries me is what kids aspire to be now. I'm going to sound hypocritical because I'm on the telly (I am also a disability advisor, so I feel like I'm allowed to have my say), but it seems like all anyone wants to do nowadays is be famous.

When I was at school, if you asked someone what they wanted to be when they were older, they would say a vet or a teacher. But if you ask most kids now they'll say 'a Kardashian'. They look at the *TOWIE* lot and think that's where their future lies, and that all they have to do is get on a reality show and their lives will be complete.

It's the same with shows like *The X Factor* and *The Voice*. They give the terrible message that success is all about how you look. I don't think a lot of kids even bother to work hard at school now because they think they're pretty much guaranteed fame, but not everyone can be in One Direction or Little Mix.[*]

There's also this whole obsession with being American when it comes to school now. I find it weird that secondary school is now called high school and that everyone has massive proms. We weren't supposed to have a prom when I was at school but a girl won a competition in *Mizz* magazine so we got to have one. We had mocktails and a chocolate fountain and Paul Danan came along. Yes, *the* Paul Danan.

America

Don't get me wrong. I'm not slagging off America. In fact, I really like it. I did this thing called Camp America several years ago where you go and work in a camp with a load of kids for an entire summer. The camp was in Pennsylvania and I've never been anywhere where kids are praised so much just for trying. We were teaching them gymnastics and if a kid even attempted to do a star jump, everyone was clapping their hands like lunatics and shouting, 'Woo, yeah! Good job!'

None of my friends wanted to go so I went on my own. I made loads of mates and we all went travelling together afterwards.

We went to Miami, which is amazing, but it is the land of the beautiful people. We stayed opposite this proper muscle beach and while we were eating croissants for breakfast they'd

---

[*] I can say that because I'm basically in Little Mix, what with me doppelgänger.

be running around in hoodies and doing push-ups even though it was scorching hot.

We went to this club one night, which was crazy. People were hanging from the ceiling and there were stage shows and all sorts going on. We made friends with some guys who were wearing red bandanas. They were all matching so I assumed they just liked the boy-band look.

We were hungry, so the bandana lads called the waitresses over and ordered us some pizzas. They seemed to know everyone and they even took us into the VIP area. I'm so naive I didn't click on for ages they were part of this really well-known Miami mafia gang. Thank God I didn't take the piss out of their headwear.

I'd love to go to Las Vegas sometime, although I've heard they pump oxygen into the casinos and clubs so everyone stays awake. And they don't have clocks anywhere so no one knows what time it is so they carry on gambling. I want to see the Grand Canyon too. I know it's just a big hole in the ground but I still want to have a look, like.

America is so different to the UK. Americans are so competitive and I think we're quite lazy. Even in the 2012 Olympics America won gold in loads of things, and whenever we won something it was in all the lazy sports where everyone is sat down, like cycling and horse riding. We never win anything where people actually have to get off their arse, do we?*

Everyone is so over the top over in America too, and

---

* We're very good at sit-down sports aren't we? We're basically gold-medal standard at sitting down. For all the ones where it's just about trying really hard, we're basically shit, aren't we?

things are so much *bigger*. I do like the food portions, though. I'm glad we don't have them over here because my roof would have to come off if I ever needed to be hospitalized because I'd be so enormous. I went to McDonald's in New York and they asked if I wanted to 'go large'. I thought, *Fuck it*, and I got a litre of Coke. It lasted me all day. It's just bizarre.

I say *everything* is big, but the Statue of Liberty was a bit disappointing. It looks massive in the movies but we went out on a boat around it and it was tiny. I was like, 'What the hell? I feel like I could climb that.'

Holidays

If ever we go somewhere new on a night out, I like to imagine I'm on holiday somewhere to make it more exciting.

I've been on some hilarious holidays with my mates in the past. My friend Kim lives in Palma so I go and visit her every year. Last year I went for six weeks but this year I only went for three, so it was just a light visit.

She lives right near Magaluf so we go there quite a lot. I used to love it there and it's fun during the day as well as at night, but this year for some reason I felt really old. I've never felt like that before but it was like everyone had gone there for their first holiday and they were really young.

That's also a lot to do with how much Magaluf has changed. In the old days you used to look up the strip and not even be able to see the road because there were so many people, but now it's almost empty. I think the bad press it got has killed it and even on a Saturday night there are usually only about twenty people walking around.

You can't drink on the streets now and there are police patrolling around, so everyone is much more careful about how they behave.

Of course, I don't agree with what went on there with girls doing sexual things for drinks and that, but it is a totally different place now. A lot of the hotels are all-inclusive, so if people go on holiday there they won't bother to leave the complex because it's all free booze. People like Tinie Tempah go out and perform in the big complexes so there's no need to leave where you're staying.

I went to Benidorm with Sam and Kelly last summer but I don't think I'd ever go back. It's too scruffy even for me and I love a bit of cheese. I don't want to sound snobby but I felt like I was in an episode of *Jeremy Kyle*. I went when I was about fourteen with my parents and really enjoyed it because we went to the old town, which is lovely, but the main holiday part felt really seedy. There were middle-aged married women going up to young blokes and trying to pull them and people having arguments in the street and I didn't love it.*

Why is it that people feel like anything goes when they're on holiday? It's like people think it's OK to break the law or act like a knobhead because they're in a different country.

I tend to try to be much cooler when I dance on holiday. I don't know why. Maybe it's to do with the sun, but I really try and pull out the moves. There are always poles in bars abroad and I turn into a pole-dancer version of Beyoncé. I have to

---

* A good rule of thumb is, if there's lots of signs up saying 'proper gravy' it's probably not going to be a very nice place.

literally be dragged off them. I think poles are a really good prop. It's almost like dancing with another person, isn't it?

We always end up going swimming in the sea after a night out. Can you imagine doing that here? You'd freeze your arse off.

My worst thing is walking back to the hotel with a kebab after a big night out and passing families who are on their way to the beach. I always feel dead guilty. My little sister is never, ever going on a girls' holiday. In fact, she's never going to be allowed to drink.

It makes me laugh that tourists expect everyone to be able to talk English when they go abroad. Even if they're in the middle of Turkey they get narked off if the locals don't understand them perfectly. It's not like we speak Turkish to people who come on holiday to Britain. It's ridiculous how often I see people talking really loudly or slowly to staff in restaurants because they think it will help them understand, and then they'll start pointing at things on the menu instead. Can you imagine if someone came up to you at work and started pointing to everything they wanted? You'd think they were losing it.

I think, generally, Brits learn about three words when they go to another country, and they're 'hello', 'thank you' and 'wine'. I know 'Uno Fanta limón and vodka, *por favor*', which gets me through whenever I go to Spain. There are also universal hand actions for things like 'drink', 'ketchup' and 'chips', which come in handy. And, of course, numbers are quite easy.

Holiday clothes

Summer is all about layering for me. Some people put loads of effort into being fit for the summer and it's great if you want to wear bikinis and little dresses, but I stay in the shade anyway, so I'm not bothered if I wear something floaty.

I'll get a spray tan before I go away and then stay out of the sun. I'm already glowing on the outward plane journey and people are dead jealous. Why risk getting burnt and sweating horribly when you don't need to? I totally skip that awkward red and white stage and go straight to brown.

I used to get disheartened when I went on holiday and worked really hard to get a natural tan and thought I was dead brown. Then you'd get into the airport light and be like, 'Is that it?' Then by the time your flight's landed back in the UK you're pale again. But not if you fake it.

The sun is so ageing too. I put sun cream on my hands and my back even when it's cloudy because I read something saying that's what ages you. I want to look eighteen for ever!

Butlin's

There's no need to go abroad at all, is there? I absolutely love going to Butlin's. I feel like I'm in *Dirty Dancing* when I'm there. You still get wake-up calls and things, and you can drive around on buggies and it's so cute.

I used to go with my family when I was growing up and it was like the centre of the universe. They had a jungle gym and it was so much fun.

I remember my granddad Tommy falling off a bar stool

once because he was really drunk, and everyone rushed over to help him. He was really annoyed because people thought he'd fallen because he was old, but it was just too much booze.

Time to go

We'll usually spend a couple of hours at someone's house before we finally venture out. We get a bit carried away because we're having such a good time, and, before we know it, it's 11 p.m. and it's time to go.

We never, ever go out before then. Nowhere gets good until after 11 p.m. and it would be weird if we went out earlier. If we went to a bar at, say, 9 p.m. it would feel like a day session. Even in my home town, which isn't very big, everywhere is open until 4 a.m., so the later you go out the later you can stay out. Everyone loves drinking where I'm from. We excel in it.

It's generally Kelly who will decide when it's time to call a taxi. I'm useless because I'll always offer to call us one but it feels like too much effort when you're drinking, so I never get around to it. I know that if I leave it long enough someone else will do it.

We always try and get Dan the Taxi Man to pick us up. He's the first person we call. We're not even totally sure if he's a real taxi driver but he's got a really big van and he's really cheap. I'm sure he only just covers the cost of petrol when he drives us places. Six of us can go to Blackpool and back for around £35 – and that's at least a two-hour drive – so I don't know how he makes any money.

We'll also ask for lifts off people quite a lot. Sam does this really annoying thing where she puts a message on Facebook saying, 'Who's doing lifts tonight?' and then she waits for people to offer. People will often post taxi numbers under her status, but sometimes she comes up trumps and someone will offer to drive us. Even if only a couple of us get a lift it's a real help. There are usually a hardcore six of us, so if two people get a lift the rest of us can get a taxi for four and we've got more money to spend on drinks.

7

SCARLETT SAYS

. . . time to move on to the pre-drinks

Scarlett's Favourite Random Facts

The Romans used to clean and whiten their teeth with wee.

An average lead pencil will write around 50,000 words.

Hot water is heavier than cold water.

Once we've had the pre-pre-drinks, it's time for the pre-drinks in the taxi, and even though I'll have been the last person to arrive, I'm the one who's shouting at everyone to hurry up and get in the taxi. My friends are always telling me to pipe down when I'm trying to take control of the situation. Everyone's like, 'Don't you dare.'

Sarah is always really prepared when it comes to the pre-drinks in the taxi. She'll get a load of those cans of spirits and mixers for us to share on the way. Some of us are not so classy and just finish whatever we've got left in our bottle.

I'm really bad when it comes to mixing my drinks. I'll have a glass of wine at home, then I'll have pre-mixed cocktails or wine for my pre-pre-drinks and while we're in the taxi, and then when I'm out, I'll always have a couple of Jack Daniel's and Cokes because I think it makes me look hard.

If it's a really bad drinking night, I'll start drinking red wine again at about 2 a.m. Even while I'm ordering it I'm thinking, *Why am I doing this?* Once I've had red wine on top of everything else I've drunk, I'm away with the showfolk. I could literally join a circus I think I'm so good at dancing.

Binge drinking

There are all these stories about binge drinking and I've always assumed that means drinking cans of cider on the morning bus, but I was really shocked the other day when I saw what the definition of binge drinking is. It's not drinking in the week, then at the weekend having more than three pints of beer if you're a man or two glasses of wine if you're a woman. So now I'm pro binge-drinking. It's basically just another word for having a weekend, isn't it? Sorry if that's not PC, but that's what I think. The media have jumped all over it and made out that it's a thing about this generation and that Britain is 'a nation of binge drinkers'. But are you telling me men were drinking less than three pints on a Friday night in the past, or that women in Paris are drinking less than two glasses of wine when they're out? I mean, even Jesus liked wine, didn't he? And he walked on water.*

I think it's because so many people take it to extremes when they get drunk and come falling out of nightclubs and fighting in the street. But I think people meeting up with their friends and having a drink on the weekend is a British tradition and we shouldn't get rid of it. When you get people

---

* Not at the same time. That would have been dangerous, like under the influence. The wine into water and walking on water are pretty impressive. But he doesn't really follow it up with any medium-sized stunts in the middle, does he? That's like the little tricks that someone does at the beginning of the show. He needed to follow that up with a few bigger illusions. There's quite a lot of general healing if I remember. Though I guess the whole coming back from the dead thing is a bit of a show-stopper. I wonder if anyone's ever done a Jesus-themed magic show. That's probably in poor taste.

coming from other countries they're really into going to the pub because it's part of our culture. It is pretty shocking when you go to the doctor's, though, and they ask you how many units a week you drink and everyone does the same thing of working out a number of drinks they think is small enough and they still say you need to cut down.

I don't often feel embarrassed if I've woken up and drunk too much, as I would never be violent. People say to me, 'You said so and so and you dance like a nutter,' but I don't care. I'll have people messaging me on Facebook saying, 'It was lovely talking to you last night,' and I don't even remember seeing them, but I'm sure we had a nice time. So what? I enjoyed it at the time. As long as I can untag myself from the embarrassing photos on social media it didn't happen.

I don't really drink a lot at home during the week, although I will on a Saturday night if I'm staying, in because me mam likes a drink too. She drinks Smirnoff Ice like a teenager. When I go to Asda she'll ask me to get her a party box and I'll be like, 'But we're not having a party. Why do you want so much?' She just loves to know that she can go and get one while she's watching *Strictly Come Dancing*, I reckon. It's the excitement of it all.

Taxis

Once we're in the taxi on the way to a bar or pub, anything goes. We tend to talk about anything and everything and Dan the Taxi Man probably knows most of our secrets by now. When you're drunk you don't care, do you? It's bad enough on the journey there but he picks us up too so we're usually mortal by then and being louder than ever. I swear we all think he's deaf or something, but he's sat right next to us hearing every word.

One of us once told a story about how she kept having green poos. She couldn't work out why and we were googling it in the car and poor Dan the Taxi Man had to listen to every little detail. We also come up with the best ideas *ever* when we're drunk. We've thought up some cracking business propositions, and we've discussed the possibility of starting our own girl band many times. Dan the Taxi Man has even offered to be our manager. Needless to say as soon as we're sober again it becomes clear they're the shittest ideas in the world and a clothing range for people who like dressing up as their pets won't *actually* sell terribly well.*

We also sing quite a lot in taxis and when I'm drunk I genuinely think I'm good. I'll be singing my heart out like I'm on *The X Factor* and the taxi driver is Simon Cowell, and this is my one chance to impress him. Sometimes when we arrive at the first bar, if we're still singing to a song we like we'll make the taxi driver wait until it's finished. How bad is that?

Secrets

Even though we clearly don't mind Dan the Taxi Man hearing all of our secrets, when it comes to other people's I'm really good at keeping them to myself. I think that's so important

---

* Actually, that one still does work. We could call it Pet-a-Porter. That's mint.

when you're friends with someone. You've got to be able to trust each other.

Having said that, some things are fair game, and I do think people are a bit stupid if they reckon I'm not going to tell Sarah most of the things I hear. When someone says to you, 'Promise not to tell anyone,' that obviously does apply, but there's also a clause that you can still tell your best friend. You have to tell one person. It's the law.

Sarah knows a lot of secrets that I've been told, and vice versa. But we would never tell anyone else, and the person whose secret it is doesn't know we've told each other. Is this making any sense? So, basically, I am good at keeping secrets except from one person, because Sarah and I do pretty much share everything.

It's always funny when someone has told me or Sarah something and then they feel like it's time to reveal their secret to the rest of the group. They'll think they're telling us something really explosive but Sarah and I will look at each other and kind of smile because we both know it already.

Sometimes people will tell me a secret and I think, *That's not even a good one*. And they'll bring it up a few months later and it's so rubbish I'll already have forgotten it. On the flip side, I love it when I'm drinking with Sarah and all of a sudden I remember a really good secret that someone's told me when I've been very drunk. It suddenly comes back to me and I feel like my head is going to explode if I don't tell Sarah right away. It reminds me of the TV show *That's So Raven*, where she sees the future and kind of zones out for a minute. I do that but I see the past and remember someone telling me something amazing. It's like getting a really fantastic surprise present or something. I love it.

I'm a bit boring because I don't really have any secrets. I'm kind of like an open book and I don't have anything interesting to keep from my mates. The biggest secret I had was when I knew I was going to be on *Gogglebox*. I wasn't allowed to tell anyone, but of *course* I had to tell some of my friends because I totally trust them.

In the past if someone's boyfriend has tried it on with me, which sadly has happened, I've been really honest about it and told my friend straight away, so then it's not a secret any more. I hadn't done anything wrong and I think it needed to be said for the sake of my mate. So basically, any kind of secrets I have come spilling out because I can't help myself, so I have nothing left to hide.

While I'm good with secrets, I think gossip is totally different and it's there to be enjoyed. If it's not hurtful or going to cause trouble, it's fair game. There are certain jobs that people do where people think you're a therapist. If you do people's hair or nails you pretty much know all of their secrets.

There's an unwritten rule that we never gossip about people in our friendship group, though. I always think that if someone will go behind someone else's back and talk about them, they'll do the same to me. It's such a warning sign. I think it's part of the reason we're such good friends. I would be really wary if someone in the group slagged off someone else in the group to me. I wouldn't be able to trust them.

A not so brief interlude on lads and lasses

Of course when you're out with the girls on a night out, lads always come into it. They can't not, can they? But honestly, I'm not usually on the lookout when I'm having fun with my friends.* When I was at uni I was much more excited about the possibility of meeting a lad and it was like it was my sole reason for going out. I always thought I was going to meet the love of my life. But these days I don't give a shit!

I would always rather be single than go out with someone just because I *think* I should be with someone. Loads of girls think if they get with someone their life is going to be perfect. Your life should be perfect anyway, and if you get together with someone, that should be an added bonus. Being single isn't a disease!

I have had boyfriends and they're not all they're cracked up to be. I mean, one day it would be nice to meet someone, but it's not my main goal in life. I'll probably end up being about fifty with loads of dogs and cats, but until that happens I'm not going to worry.

I'd like a Sunday boyfriend for when I'm hungover and feel shit, but that's about it. Someone should start a business where you can hire a part-time boyfriend for a Sunday night.

---

* Although I do have one tip that Sam does and it always works. Wear an 'It's my 50th' badge. I don't know why it works but it's like some sort of magnet where she ends up with ten different mobile numbers by the end of the night. To be fair, it could be that they're all obsessed with cougars and think, *'Bah, she looks well for her age'*. We've not done the maths to see whether if you wear a 60th badge you get more numbers, and I'll leave that to one of you to experiment with.

They can come over around lunchtime and then leave about 9 p.m. and be like, 'See you next Sunday!' That would suit me.

My resistance to meeting lads on a night out could be partly because I kind of think blokes wouldn't fancy me then anyway. Any guy who finds me attractive after six wines (drunk by me, not him) is seriously seeing me through rose-tinted beer glasses. I am in no way attractive when I'm throwing myself around a dance floor singing along to Katy Perry at the top of my voice. No lad is going to get a look-in when I'm locked up in my prison of drunken dance.

Ten things not to say to a single person

1) 'Don't worry (not that I was anyway), you'll meet someone when you're least expecting it.'
What does that even mean? Is the love of my life going to jump out from under my bed with a bouquet of flowers when I try to go to sleep tonight? Because I'm not expecting that.

2) 'Do you ever feel lonely?'
Just because you're single doesn't mean you're lonely, just the same as being in a relationship doesn't necessarily mean you're happy.

3) 'Have you ever tried an online dating site like Tinder or Plenty of Fish?'
Have you ever tried minding your own business?

4) 'Maybe you should cross a few of the qualities you want your future husband to have off your list to give yourself a better chance?'

I've waited this long, mofo, I'm not compromising on anything.

5) 'Maybe you're looking in the wrong places?'

Oh, so I should be looking in local prisons for prospective boyfriends? No wonder it hasn't been working out.

6) 'But how are you even single?'

Because I don't just go out with any old idiot. Being single can be a life choice, you know.

7) When friends organize a couple's night out: 'I mean, you could come, but it will be all couples.'

Don't panic, you're not going to catch singledom.

8) My parents: 'You won't find a boyfriend at the bottom of a wine bottle.'

No, but I will find that it helps me have a good time and dance like Beyoncé.

9) At a wedding: 'This will be you one day.'

Yeah, all I need to do first is find someone, get them to want to spend the rest of their life with me, and then book a wedding.

10) 'You are such a catch. Someone will snatch you up.'

I KNOW!

Drink etiquette

If a lad offers to buy me a drink and I do want to accept, I'll always go to the bar with them and watch them buy it, or I'll ask for the money and get it myself. Seriously, I do. Or I'll say, 'You give me the money and I'll go and get us both one.' It's because I'm a bit paranoid about my drink being spiked ever since my friend's was when I was at uni. I can't believe people do that to other people. What's wrong with the world? It scares me that it happens so often people don't seem to take it that seriously any more.

My type of lad

I definitely have a type when it comes to lads, and it's not bloody One Direction. All of my ex-boyfriends look the same. They have to have dark hair – I've never been out with a blond or ginger lad in my life – and they need to be quite tanned. And obviously they have to be taller than me because I'm only 5ft. They should also be quite well built, but where I live, as I've said, there aren't many guys who don't go to the gym to be fair. My final stipulation is that they dress like knobheads. I don't know why but I seem to like guys who wear tight jeans with turn-ups and loafers with no socks. Why do I do it? I know before I dive in what I'm doing. I'm well aware they're going to be dickheads but I can't help myself. It's like in nature when certain animals are brightly coloured to warn you they're dangerous.

Me ideal man

I get so much stick for this from my mates, but I find Simon Cowell really attractive. Even though he has slight man boobs and that. He's just really attractive. It must be the power thing. Also, if he said something nice about you, you'd know he meant it. 'Hello, Simon love, what do you think of my new top?'

'I think it's ugly, garish and you look like a whore.'

That's why I'm single, because I can't find anyone like that round my way.

My other crush is Stephen Hawking. Similarly, it's such a pain for him to say stuff that if he was like, 'You look nice,' you'd know he meant it.

Me mates all think I'm weird. I'd go out with Stephen Hawking. If he was younger. We're on different paths. I said that to a friend and she was like, 'Yeah, that's the only reason you wouldn't get together?' You'd smash the pub quiz as well, wouldn't you? Or maybe you wouldn't. It takes him quite a while to program new stuff in but if it was multiple choice you'd be well in.

I've set up a right tussle there, haven't I? Hawking and Cowell in a duel, and you can probably throw Bieber in there as well.

I think they all have something about them.

Mind you, I get annoyed with the idea of types sometimes. You know that thing people used to say: 'Are you a leg man or a boob man?' and some people would actually have an answer. Or when they do phone-ins and ask you who your celebrity crush is and people phone up and say, 'Brad Pitt.'

That's just a waste of a vote. That's like saying your favourite thing is oxygen or water or something. Pick someone a bit interesting, man. I'm not saying phone in and be like, 'Hitler,' but put a bit of thought into it.

Beards

I used to quite like beards before every lad in the world started having one. It used to be cool, but I've got beard blindness now. Everyone looks the fucking same. You walk into a pub and all the lads look like the penguins in the enclosure at the zoo. You can never tell what their faces look like in real life. I feel sorry for men who had beards before they got trendy because they've been totally ruined.

I think when beards properly go out of fashion there are going to be loads of break-ups because all these women are going to realize they've been going out with ugly men. What if they've got a properly massive chin? Or worse, no chin at all? My mate was dating this guy who looked really cool with a beard. He had what I call a pube beard because it was dead curly, but it really suited him. Then one day he shaved it off and when he walked into the pub we were all like, 'Who the fuck is that?' because he had the queerest-shaped head. It was like a little peanut. By that point my mate loved him so she didn't mind, but it would be a deal breaker for a lot of women.

I read that there are more germs in a beard than on a toilet seat, and I can imagine that's true. And the worst thing is that horrible scratching sound they make when you touch them. That makes me feel like vomiting when I think about it.

I still like stubble on a man, but I'm not a fan of those

beards that look like a kid's drawn them on, or Santa beards. They're a bit over the top. And I'm sick of guys walking round in checked shirts and beards looking like lumberjacks. Throw in a man bun and you've got my worst nightmare. It just screams 'twat'. It's not OK for a man to wear his hair in a bun. It's just *not*.

There are all these videos on the internet of kids crying when their dad has shaved his beard off.

Metrosexuals

I don't get the whole hipster thing generally. Even five years ago lads used to be lads. I'm all for equality but some of them take it too far. I saw a lad in Boots the other day buying a face pack and I was praying it was for his girlfriend. It's nice that men take care of themselves but I never want to go out with a lad who a) wears more make-up than me, or b) has better eyebrows than me. That's not how life works. I want a man to say to me, 'Why do you spend so long doing your bloody eyebrows?' not, 'Can I borrow your tweezers?' My ex used to borrow my bronzer and now I look back on it and think, *What the actual fuck?* Time is a great teacher, and it's taught me that was in *no way* OK.

Exes

I had my first ever proper boyfriend when I was sixteen. He was fifteen but he was the hardest lad in school, so everyone fancied him. He came home and he was bigger than my dad and he had tattoos. I think me mam was immediately a bit less excited about my first boyfriend. I remember her saying, 'He looks like Herman Munster.'

I tried to get him into *Blackadder* and that but he wasn't interested.

Looks aside, I really want to meet a lad who is funny, and I'm yet to meet a guy who actually makes me laugh. When I've gone out with men before I generally only end up laughing if I've done something stupid and I'm laughing at myself, rather than because they've been rolling out the one-liners.

No, hang on, I did have a funny date *once*. I went out with this one lad for a while and on our third date we went to his dad's garage because he had to pick something up. It was glass-fronted, and while we were there we superglued some pound coins to the ground outside and watched people walk past and try to pick them up. That was his idea and it was actually hilarious. Apart from that, the craic's been pretty shit with my exes.

I was with one lad for about three years and I said to my friend Sarah that something was missing from our relationship but I couldn't work out what. I was seeing him that night and she told me to let him talk first and see if he could hold his own. We were sat at his house watching TV and I decided to stay silent – and so did he. After an hour I said, 'You're quiet?' and he said, 'Well, you're not talking.' I looked at him and said, 'This isn't working, is it?' And that was the main reason we split up. I was bored of being a performing monkey.

The crazy thing was I thought things were going really well and I didn't even realize I was making all the effort. Then I saw other couples having a laugh with each other and it really hit me. My mam said a while after we broke up that she'd never once had a conversation with him, and she was so right. I was wrapped up in this big bubble and as soon as it popped I could see everything so clearly. They say love is blind, and I could have done with about eight guide dogs when I was in that relationship.

I was with another lad who was so boring I used to look into the future and I already knew what it was going to be like. If we went out on a Saturday, we would go to one of two places and it was so predictable. I was in serious danger of turning into a fifty-year-old when I was twenty-one.

My friends used to call one ex boyfriend of mine Keith Lard after the character from *Phoenix Nights* because he was obsessed with his dog. He had a Great Dane and I started to think he fancied it. It always came first. It used to jump up at me and nearly knock me over and instead of telling it off he used to say, 'Isn't he cute? I think he likes you.'

The final straw was when we were supposed to go out for New Year and he couldn't get a dog-sitter so he wanted to stay in instead. It was at that point I realized I couldn't be second best to a dog.

I went out with a proper mammy's boy once – the same one who was at uni while I was at school – and for quite a long time too. I planned for us to go to York one New Year and go to The Olive Tree, which is the nicest restaurant there. His parents had a place nearby where he said we could stay, but when he came to pick me up his mam and dad were in the car and they came on the entire date with us.

His parents used to pay for lots of things for him. He was so spoilt. When I went round their house once his mam asked me if I knew how to use a knife and fork because of where I'm from. I mean, I do live in a different area to them and I don't have any airs and graces but I am aware of how cutlery works! She also asked what benefits my parents were on and seemed genuinely surprised when I said they both work.

His dad used to pour out expensive wine and say to me, 'Sip it and taste it, Scarlett, don't down it. It cost £35.' I didn't give a shit. I'd have happily gone down the shop and bought some Echo Falls. I don't know how I didn't walk out of his house on several occasions.

One time we were showing his mam our holiday photos and I was smoking a shisha pipe, which is basically flavoured water. She started saying to him, 'Is this the type of woman you want raising your kids?' like I was a liability!

My mam said to me one day, 'If you spend the rest of your life with him, she'll be picking out your curtains and all sorts. Get out while you can!' In the end his mam actually ended it for us. I didn't even get a phone call from him. She rang me and said he didn't want to be with me any more.

He came and picked up his stuff and dropped mine off and that was it. I didn't even feel sad because I thought, *If you don't have the balls to actually split up with me, I've had a lucky escape.*

I learnt a lot from him and he taught me not to make someone your everything.

I also once went out with this lad whose dad owned a prestige car dealership. He turned up in a Ferrari and my dad looked out the window and just said, 'Nope.' And I asked him what did he mean and he said, 'I know I keep telling you to go out with people that want to make something of themselves but that fella out there's a prick.' Dads just have a sixth sense, don't they?

I had a boyfriend in my final year at school who was in his second year of university. It's that man thing, though, isn't it, of half your age plus seven. Why is it OK for men to be with much younger women? I suppose it's because men can have children basically till they die. They can ponce about for ever.

Strippers

I went out with a stripper for a year and a half and he used to get us to tan his back. He'd get a lot of messages on Facebook from the women he'd been out with. I don't understand all these people who show how much they're in the gym. You should pretend it's effortless – that's cool. He wore all those really low-cut T-shirts with the he-vage and sleeve tattoos. He'd set his alarm to wake up in the middle of the night to eat cottage cheese, so he'd build more muscle. And he'd go on at me to get fit. He'd be like, 'Do you think you should be eating that?' and I'd reply, 'Yes, because it's fucking delicious.' 'But you're getting a bit chubby,' he'd say, and I'd say, 'Look at this face – zero fucks given.'

He also wore a headband quite a lot. I look back now and can't believe we went out. I get photos from him popping up every now and then in my timeline where he's got someone at the gym to take a photograph of him while he's working out.

Dates

I have been on some really dodgy dates in my time. My friend met a guy on Tinder and she set me up on a date with his mate – just as her and the other lad split up. He took me to this Italian restaurant in Sunderland, and when we got there one of his exes was there, so he kept turning round and looking at her. We had nothing in common and there were so many silences we were both constantly going to the toilet just so we had something to do.

On the taxi journey home we burst out laughing because it had been such a bad night and it kind of broke the ice, but then he started slagging off my mate! It was a good forty-five-minute drive home so it was *very* awkward. About halfway back I remembered I didn't have a key to my house so I called my friend Bam and asked if I could stay at hers so I didn't wake my mam and dad up. I found out later that my 'date' had told everyone I'd got dropped off at another lad's house. He was saying to people, 'Yeah, she went on a date with me and then went back to another bloke's house.' Cheeky git.

Another time I went out on a few dates with a lad who was a doorman and security guard. I usually think they're knobheads, but he was such a lovely guy I thought I'd make the effort. One day I couldn't make one of our dates because I was ill and he sent me a massive bouquet of flowers. I had to finish with him because it was so over the top. How bad is that? I finished with a lad just because he bought me flowers. What's wrong with me?

I feel like going for food is quite a shitty date. You don't want to look too greedy, but you don't want to look like you don't eat. You have to be really careful what you order. You can't have spaghetti bolognaise because it splashes about, and you can't have garlic because you'll stink.

This is really bad, but if I go on a date to a restaurant I'll eat before I go so I don't look like a massive glutton. Even so, I would never order a salad in a restaurant. I don't see the point if you're eating out.

I once went on a date with a guy and when it came to ordering he said, 'Ladies first.' I knew he was paying so I was like fuck it and I ordered a steak. Then when it was his turn to order he asked for a bloody pear and walnut salad. I was like, what the fuck? He wasn't even vegetarian. When the waitress brought the food over she gave me the salad and him the steak and it was so embarrassing. We didn't have a second date.

I went out with this lad who's played rugby for England, so he's a bit of a celeb round our way. I used to date him in school and one night when we were out he asked me if he could take me for food the following week. I got dressed up thinking we were going to a restaurant, and he took me to the KFC drive-through.

He actually asked me if I wanted to sit in or eat in the car. That was the extent of the romance. Not surprisingly, I turned down his offer of a second date, and he texted me a while later saying, 'I can see where I went wrong now.' Which bit? When I had to sit in the car eating beans with a plastic fork? Or when you made me listen to the radio while I ate my chips as we drove off?

When I was at uni, I put a really miserable post on Facebook after a night out about what a shit evening I'd had. This guy I knew from home saw it and travelled all the way to York at 5 a.m. to surprise me as a romantic gesture. How awkward was that? Sarah felt sorry for him so she let him sleep on the couch but it was hardly the staircase scene from *Pretty Woman*, was it? I think he thought it would win me over, but the stumbling block was that I didn't fancy him.

I feel like going to the cinema is a great date. A lot of people don't like it, but you can chat all the way there, and then on the way home you've got something to talk about so you don't run out of things to say.

Some of my better dates have been to places like York Dungeons or playing mini golf. I love it if a lad is a bit inventive. Netflix and food is *not* a date. If a lad invites me over to theirs for dinner or to watch a film before date five, that's it. If they can't be arsed to take me out by then, what chance have we got? My friends say I expect too much from a lad but I don't think I do. The first six months at least should be *really* exciting and they should be trying to win you over. As soon as you say yes to going round there to watch a movie they'll think that's OK and they won't make an effort any more. Some girls want to get into a relationship and get settled down and secure as soon as possible, but I don't. I want excitement.

My friend Billy once went on a date with a lad who owned a few houses, but halfway through the date someone wanted to view one of them so he took her with him to meet them. Then he said, 'We're really near my house so I may as well introduce you to my dog,' and he made her take the dog for a walk in the local graveyard with him.

When she went inside his house for a coffee he had loads

of taxidermied animals everywhere. She had to text me so I could call her and pretend to be her mam so she could make her escape. I guess it's always good to find out early on if someone is a bit weird.

The girls and I have always got each other's backs on dates. If one is going badly, we'll slip away to the toilet and text someone asking them to call and give us a good get-out.

I don't always tell my mam when I'm going on dates because she really gets her hopes up and I hate disappointing her if I don't like someone. She always says to me, 'Do you think he's the one?' before I've even been on the date.

The worst thing someone could do on a date is clack their food or slurp their drink. I don't just mean it irritates me a bit, it actually makes my heart hurt. I can feel myself getting really angry. If my mam rings me on her break at work and she's slurping her tea, I have to put the phone down. And that's my own *mam*. It's a million times worse with strangers. That's a relationship deal-breaker for me.

I'm quite traditional and it never offends me when a guy holds a door open for me or asks me what I want to drink or eat before they order. I think it's gentlemanly. I think it depends what your dad's like. Me dad is a proper gentleman so I don't see why anyone else shouldn't be. But I've got no time for someone telling me what to eat and drink. Like in *Titanic*, man, when Billy Zane tells the waiter what Kate Winslet's going to have for dinner. I was too young to see that at the cinema, but I reckon you could hear the groan go round from all the women. That's someone straight on the shitlist.

Drunk dates

Drunk dates can be both good and bad. It's helpful to find out if a lad is a knob when he's pissed, but you don't want to make a knob of yourself.

I think it's a bit dangerous to get drunk on an early date. I reckon on the fifth date you're fine to have a few, but not until then. It's never going to end well. When I think of all the embarrassing things I do when I'm drunk . . . You have to wait a while to show someone your crazy side, otherwise they'll think you're a lunatic from day one. That's the thing about early dates, isn't it? It's two people pretending to be totally normal, so they're not actually being themselves. It's not till you can be a bit mad that someone really gets to know what you're like and it becomes fun. I reckon for some people it never gets like that and they're just on their best behaviour the whole time. It must be exhausting.

Being dumped

My first rule for dumping someone it that it should never happen via email, text or phone, it should always be done face to face. My second rule is that you need a good reason. And my third rule is that you should wait a certain amount of time before you move on.

It pisses me off when people dump someone because they want space, and then two weeks later they're in another relationship.

No one likes being dumped, do they? Why would you? I've been lucky because when my relationships have finished it's been mainly mutual. I was going out with a lad at uni for about six months and I think we both realized it wasn't working so we decided to split up. About a week later he got together with someone else and I was a bit offended so (and I do know this isn't rational) I sold a pair of his shorts and a hoodie from American Apparel on eBay, and then I sent him a screenshot of it.

I also cut up another one of his hoodies and posted it back in pieces through his letterbox. This lad and I laugh about it now because we're still friends, but isn't it weird what break-ups can do to you? I didn't even give him the money for them, though, so I probably still owe that to him.

If I was to split up with someone these days, I would never, *ever* use the 'it's not you, it's me' crap. If you're dumping someone, of *course* it's them! I would much rather someone was honest with me, and I will also be honest with other people. I would rather someone said to me, 'I think your craic's shite.' Fair enough. Also, do it sooner rather than later so that person can go off and meet someone else.

Finally, if you weren't friends before you got together, don't try to be afterwards. It's over. It's done. Block them from all of your social media and draw a line under it. Cyber-stalking is too easy; it's tragic and you may end up discovering things you don't want to know. All of a sudden you'll find yourself looking at their posts from 2013 and realizing you've lost two hours of your life.*

---

* I've got a mate who was telling me that she was deep into stalking an ex, like in the photos of a friend's sister, because she'd forgot herself and was interested in this girl she saw in the photos and what her life was like and her computer froze and she accidentally clicked the like button. That's a

I always think it's a good idea to avoid the places you used to go together, or where you know they'll be. Don't purposely go somewhere knowing they'll be there. What good can come of that? None. Zero. And you'll look like a twat.

Scarlett translates break-up lines

I need some alone time:
I want to have sex with other people.

I don't think I'm ready for a serious relationship:
I was using you and I'm either bored or I've found someone I like better (also I'm a dickhead).

I'm going through a lot right now, it's not fair on you:
I have lots of other things that are more important than you and basically can't be arsed.

I think we need some space apart:
You are doing my tits in, leave me alone for five minutes and I might actually miss you.

The good old Rachel and Ross classic: we need a break:
I want to see if I can meet anyone better than you, if I can't, see you in a couple of months.

We've grown apart: I'm bored:
It's not you: It's obviously you.

---

nightmare, that is. How are you gonna explain what you were doing there? It's like sometimes when you see someone's Facebook status and they've just typed someone's name in because they were looking for them. Awkward!

8
SCARLETT SAYS

. . . choose a venue

Scarlett's Favourite Random Facts

Earth is the only planet not named
after a god.

Pigs can't look up at the sky.
Their body shape makes it
physically impossible.

Shakespeare made up the name
Jessica when he wrote THE
MERCHANT OF VENICE.

There isn't one person who decides where we go on a night out. We all kind of decide together. If we're going out locally, there's one big square where all of the bars are, so that's easy. We get dropped off and then we do the rounds and that's when the actual drinking starts. You know, the *real* drinking. No more of that pre shit.

We usually go to Wetherpoons, the champagne bar, The Castle Bar, back to the champagne bar, and then to Monaco's. The champagne bar is great because we know the DJ and we always ask him to put on records we love so it's like our own giant personal jukebox.

I like going to Wetherpoons because ours is a good one, but they're not allowed to play music and I once got kicked out of there because I was rapping. It was dead quiet so I thought it would be a great idea to start MC-ing when I was drunk. I stood on a table and everything. Me friends were all banging on the table like it was a drum and loads of people were joining in, but they still kicked me out. I'm not being funny but I was probably doing good business for them! Obviously, I was back in there the following week, though. It's got a good garden too, which is really nice in the summer, even if it is full of smokers . . .

Smoking

I've never, ever smoked in my life so I was really pleased when people were banned from lighting up inside, especially in eating areas. I remember having nights out and getting home and stinking of smoke. I used to have to scrub myself to get the smell out because I was like a walking ashtray.

A lot of my friends who did smoke have given up, and the ones who still do always say they're going to give up every winter because it's too cold to stand outside. But now everywhere has got bloody heat lamps to keep them warm, so they don't have to. Let smokers catch hypothermia – that'll stop them!

If any of them ask me to go outside for a fag with them if we're out, I'll always say no. If someone I want to speak to is in a smoking area, I'll go and chat to them, and it's also a great place for making new friends, but I'll never go out especially with a friend just because they want a cigarette. I don't want to encourage them in any way. They chose that path.

I do feel proud to be able to say at my age that I've never, ever even tried a fag. I was never cool enough at school for anyone to peer-pressure me, and I never wanted to try it just to fit in. Me dad and I used to write 'little cancer sticks' on me mam's fags back when she still smoked because we hated it so much. We'd hide them and everything. My dad has never smoked so he's really anti it too.

One time when I was younger I agreed to put my friend's cigarettes in my coat pocket because she wasn't wearing one and I completely forgot so I went home with them. My dad found them and he was so angry with me. I kept saying they weren't mine but in his mind of course I was going to say that. Thankfully, in the end, he believed me, but it was awful. I felt guilty even though I hadn't done anything and I ended up crying me eyes out!

I've never really got why people start smoking in the first place. All they seem to do is spend the rest of their lives trying to give up. And it costs a bloody fortune. You might as well walk outside your front door and throw money at passers-by, or burn a £10 note every time you fancy buying a packet of fags. If people smoke twenty a day, that adds up to about £280 a month. Sometimes if I buy meself something I know I shouldn't, I'll think, *Well, I don't smoke so I'm saving meself a fortune, which means I'm allowed.* If I want to buy another new top, it's fine because it only equals three packets of cigarettes.

My friends who smoke probably find me quite annoying because I'm desperate for them all to quit. When they light up I'll say, 'Ooh, that's a little bit more of your lung you're damaging there.' At the end of the day I can't force people to stop. It's got to be their choice, but I do try and help where I can, even if it does come across as a bit irritating. I don't want them all getting ill and shit. I care about them too much, and who will I go to the champagne bar with?

Electronic cigarettes

I also disagree with people smoking electronic cigarettes while I'm eating. It's no different to having a fag. People are so obsessed with them and there are shops everywhere now. I don't understand it. I heard the government were going to start giving out e-cigarettes on the NHS. I really hope that's not true. It's ridiculous.

It's being really glamorized and there are so many flavours, like pear drops and raspberry sorbet. Why would you want a fag that tastes like a dessert? What's going to be next? Cheese and onion?

They had those TV adverts a while back which made it look all sexy and they banned them, which I think is right.

Toilet friends

Like the smoking area, toilets are a goldmine for new mates on a night out. I always end up being people's best friend after a chat by the hand dryer. I'm forever saying hello to random girls when I'm out, and when my mates ask me how I know them I nearly always say, 'I met them in the loos.' They're my toilet friends.*

Venturing further afield

If my friends and I decide to go further afield than our local town on a night out, we'll generally get dropped off in the centre of somewhere – say York or Doncaster – and we'll just see where our legs take us. I love going out in Durham but everything's so spread out we have to have a bit of a plan if we go there. If we're not feeling too lazy, we'll go to the bottom end and then to the Gala at the top. It all depends on whether we can be arsed to do both. If we don't want to walk,

---

* Actually that sounds a little bit like some sort of air freshener, doesn't it?

we go straight to the Gala, which has got places like Fat Buddha, Ebony, Slug and Lettuce, Lloyds and Love Shack in it.

Love Shack is so cool. It's got an old VW camper van with a table inside and you can sit in there and have drinks. It's also got cages that you can dance in, but only idiots go in them. People always think they look really sexy in the cages, but they're usually mortal and they end up looking like zoo animals flailing around.

Random nights out

My mates and I have really random nights out sometimes, and someone suggested a while ago that we go and see the Dream Boys at Love Shack. It seemed like a great idea on paper, but in reality it was mortifying, and of course I had to get really pissed to get through it.

We all sat quite near the front of the stage and one of the strippers kept trying to drag me up to dance with him. No fucking way, mate. I think he thought I was being coy so I had to give my 'I'm really not fucking joking' face.

Another dancer was supposed to do a sexy routine with a chair, and he walked into the audience to grab one but when he tried to pick it up it was connected to about six others so they all moved together in one long row. He spent ages trying to unfasten it while the music was blaring out and we were all like, 'Come on now, the moment's gone.' In the end two blokes from the bar had to come and help him and it was *so* awkward. Everyone was pissing themselves, and when he did eventually do the dance it was the least sexy thing you've ever seen, bless him. We were supposed to fancy him but instead I felt dead sorry for him.*

A lot of my nights out are random, really. One of the most random ones was when Shannon and I went to the bingo. It cost a bloody fortune! It was hilarious and we were one number off of winning a grand. It's all electronic now so you don't have dabbers, which I was gutted about. But on the plus side they sell wine.

You know when you have those nights where you go for food and then you end up out until a stupid time and none of you know how it happened? My mates and I will end up in a club and girls will be there in bandage dresses with their hair backcombed to the ceiling and we're in jeans and jumpers.

Those nights are what I look forward to most because they create memories and we still talk about nights out we had years ago. I love impromptu nights like that. My friend Hannah and I went to curry night at Wetherspoons recently and we had so much wine and then went on to this pub called The Merry Monk that does five Jägerbombs for a fiver. We stayed out until three in the morning and we ended up dancing on the tables. That would never happen if you went out with a lad. It's not really the kind of thing you want to do with your boyfriend. They're called girls' nights out instead of ladies' nights because you do *not* act like ladies.

Some of my most random nights out are with my drag-queen friends. When I did ballroom dancing, funnily enough quite a lot of gay men did it too. We often went out to gay

---

* A little tip for you as well. Make sure if you're going to give the stripper money that you've got notes. Now is not the time to use up your change.

nights in local clubs and I met more of their friends, and now I've got a big group I hang out with. A lot of them are drag queens, and one of my really good friends, as well as his actual name, is also known as Janice Dickinyourson. He didn't do drag when I first knew him but one day he came down the stairs in a wig with massive boobs and I was like, 'OK . . .'

There's also Emma Roid, Miss Cara, Roxy Tart, Felicity Bean and our posh drag-queen friend Gucci. She's really well-to-do. I'm also really good friends with a guy, whose drag name is Tess Tickle. He teaches at a school and quite a lot of his pupils know he dresses up but they're cool with it. He's who I got me dog Bonnie Blue from.

I once went out to a gay night with some of my mates and I wore this bright red Little Mermaid wig with a teddy bear T-shirt and a see-through poncho and people thought I was a drag queen. When I told them I was a girl they were like, 'Well, we meant you're an attractive drag queen,' but it still wasn't a compliment. I would love my friends to do me up with proper drag make-up when we go out on our next Mon-gay, though. Imagine how many pairs of false eyelashes I could wear.

Queues

No one likes bloody queuing, do they? It's always the worst part of any evening. Lloyds in Durham is good for a night out but there's always a massive queue so you've either got to get there early, or hope you spot someone you know and pretend you want to have a conversation with them so you can basically push in. I'm saying that, but at the risk of sounding really twatty, I don't generally have to queue much any more. That's the power of TV! I usually tweet to say I'm going somewhere and someone will get back to me and say, 'Let us know when you're here and we'll sort you out.' The two best things about being on the telly are free alcohol and no queues.

I always think it's weird that the people who get the free alcohol are the ones who can afford it. It doesn't make any sense. Famous people get so much free shit but they've all got loads of money. Sadly I won't be buying a private island any time soon but I have noticed that really big celebrities don't have to pay for anything even though they're loaded.

If I'm feeling a bit shy, I'll get one of my mates to tweet a venue because I'm so worried about looking like I've got a big head and I'm expecting free entry. I'm friends with quite a lot of the people that run the bars we go to regularly so usually they'll invite me along anyway, but sometimes I'll get Sarah to message them so they don't get the wrong idea. I would never just turn up somewhere and expect the bloody red carpet to be rolled out. Can you imagine if you arrived with a smug grin on yourself all like, 'Yes, it's true, it's me, I'm here.' AWFUL. I cringe just thinking about it.

There have been times when I've been waiting to get into a bar and people have asked me why I'm queuing and I'm like, 'Because I'm a person.' Then they'll try and blag me in, and blag themselves in at the same time!

Clearly if someone does offer me quick entry in, I'm not stupid, I'm not going to queue, but equally I would never throw my weight around or expect anything. The day I hear someone say, 'Who the fuck does she think she is?' is the day

I properly check myself. I say that about other people so I would hate to be like that myself.

Double life

Sometimes when I'm out now I feel like I'm living a double life. I get free entry into clubs and I get asked for photos non-stop at the weekend, but obviously I have a day job as well. I'll go and do my nine-to-five all week, and then when the weekend comes I morph into Victoria Beckham. I look like I can't be arsed from Monday to Friday, and then on a Saturday I'll get my nails done and maybe get a blow-dry and all of a sudden I'm fucking Rihanna. I think it's cos now if I didn't make an effort then people would tweet about it and they'd probably @ me in as well so I'd read it. 'Saw Scarlett looking minging this weekend.' Cheers.

It's dead weird that everyone wants to talk to me and buy me drinks on a night out. I'll have a weekend of selfie-ing my arse off with people, and then come Monday morning I'll have to get up at 6 a.m. and go and sit behind a desk for eight hours. It's a proper crash down to reality.

Table whores

One thing I can't stand on a night out is table whores. It seems to happen a lot in Newcastle, where people try to make friends with other people if they've got a table and free booze in a club. If I go out with my mates, I stick with them for the evening. I'm not interested in sucking up to someone so I can sit at their table and try and blag some bloody vodka. Some people will make friends with anyone if they think there's something in it for them, and they'll just leave their mates to their own devices. They properly pimp themselves out.

There are also people who use other people's names to get into places. They're so blatant about it. They're all like, 'I know so and so, and my mate knows them too.' So what? I met Tom Jones when I was nine but I'm not asking for free tickets to his concert.*

Being recognized

I think I've got one of those faces that's quite recognizable, and the tan probably doesn't help, so I do get spotted quite a lot. Sometimes people will just randomly shout my name out or bellow 'Gogglebox' at me. I think that's quite strange. If I saw someone from *EastEnders*, I wouldn't shout 'EastEnders' at the top my voice and start singing the theme tune.

A lot of people also shout 'Gogglehead' instead of 'Gogglebox', or say to me, 'You're that girl out of *Gogglebox*,' as if I don't know! Admittedly, I have pretended to be someone else before too. Sometimes when people ask me if I'm Scarlett from *Gogglebox* I'll say, 'No, but I get that a lot. I'm going to have to start watching that show.'

Another odd thing people do is ask for photos even though they don't know who I am. They'll see loads of other people asking for pictures so they join in, but they haven't got

* Although if anyone from Mr Jones's team is reading, I did feel like we got on very well, so if there are any spare tickets floating about, I'd love to go.

a clue why they're getting a selfie with me. I'll say to them, 'Do you watch the show? Who's your favourite?' and they'll reply, 'What show?' There's nowt as queer as folk. I didn't realize how strange people were until I was on telly. There are a lot of nutters out there.

I saw someone go up to a guy from a TV show at a train station recently and ask for a photo with them, and the 'celebrity' turned around and told them to fuck off. I was fuming. Even if someone is the fiftieth person to ask you for a photo that day, they don't know they are. They probably think they're the first person to ask you, and it takes two seconds to be nice.

The thing that freaks me out is when people tag me in photos on Twitter or Facebook even though I haven't seen them take one. It'll be a picture of me sitting drinking with my mates and someone else in the bar will have taken it without me knowing. I find that dead creepy. I don't let the fact that random people are taking secret photos of me get in the way of a good night out, though, and I still act and dance like a twat. It's what a night out is for, isn't it?

Fake friends

I try not to be suspicious of people, because I like to give everyone a fair chance, but I am aware that some people just want to be mates with me because I'm on TV. I am pretty good at spotting it when it happens, though, and I know who my real friends are.

Quite often people I haven't seen for ages, and who would have walked past me in the street two years ago, will say to me, 'Do you remember the time we did so and so when we were seven?' and then ask for my number. I'm pretty upfront about not giving my number out. Sometimes I'll make a joke about someone potentially being a mass murderer, and other times I'll just say I don't want to. I don't want to look like I'm being arsey, but equally I don't want loads of random people I don't know texting me. Who does?

Sometimes I'll hide my phone on a night out because otherwise you've got no excuse, and I have given fake numbers to people before. The best thing to do is say your real number but change just one digit. That's my usual trick and it works. Unless I'm too pissed, and then it gets dead confusing.

What's in my handbag?

Always a pair of eyelashes and some spare glue

They're a necessity. If ever the pollen count is high or you go and see a sad film, your eyelashes get ruined, so you should always have a spare pair.

My phone

For emergencies, Twitter, Facebook, and also if I need to take a photo and put it on Instagram.

ID

I literally look twelve and often get ID'd when I'm buying things like razors and party poppers. I once got ID'd for plastic cutlery. Because if you're going to stab someone, it's clearly going to be with a plastic knife.

Contactless card

I never tend to keep money in me bag because of a tragic incident where I threw £20 out, thinking it was a receipt. I'm still bitter.

Phone charger

Because iPhone batteries last about an hour, and I may need to make an emergency call. Or send a good tweet.

Bronzer and bronzer brush

For obvious reasons!

Tangle Teezer and hairspray

Because when you have a lion's mane it needs brushing at least five times a day.

Dancing

Once we're inside a bar or club I properly go for it on the dance floor. I swear, I think I'm a member of Diversity when I'm drunk. I'll do a bit of everything, from hip-hop to robotics, and I'll try and get my friends to copy me. How geeky is that? Funnily enough, they rarely do.

I think anything goes when it comes to dancing. I love doing the worm on a night out even though I'm really shit at it. My friends and I have actual dance moves to certain songs and we think we're mint when we've been drinking. But if I'm being brutally honest, none of us are good dancers. We do a lot of lunges, squats and jogging on the spot. It looks like we're doing an aerobics class and it's the only time I actually do any gym moves. If some of my friends are at the bar and some are on the dance floor, we'll all look at each other and lunge at the same time. It may look ridiculous but it's the funniest thing, and sometimes other random people will join in. I love it when that happens.

My technique is to move my feet and hope my arms do something good on their own. I like to dance until I drop. It makes you feel really good. I think dancing gives you the same high as you get when you eat chocolate. It's my main reason for going out and it doesn't matter how shit your day at work has been, dancing makes you feel amazing.

I've danced on a lot of tables over the years, and the occasional bar. I usually get told to get down, but for that brief moment I'm up there I'm Britney, bitch. All the really posey people will look at me like I'm an idiot, but I don't care. If they've got time to look at me like I'm being a twat, they're obviously not having a very good night!

Not many men can dance and it's so embarrassing when they think they're good but they're not. There was a real trend for lads shuffling a while back and it looked bloody ridiculous. You'd go out and every fucker would be on the dance floor shuffling and they looked deranged. They'd have these big chunky trainers on and they'd be literally shuffling around the floor like dickheads, all doing exactly the same moves in a pack. I honestly think they thought they looked cool. I mean, it's hardly going to become a 'thing' on *Strictly*, is it? We're not going to hear Len Goodman saying, 'Well done, thingy from *Holby City*, you've done some quality shuffling there,' any time soon.

Also, if you like a lad and he's doing the shuffle, how are

you supposed to make a move? You can't really go up and start shuffling next to him, can you?

I do like it if lads dance funny, though. I think if a bloke can take the piss out of themselves and he doesn't mind dancing like a twat, he's probably a funny person. I like anyone who can laugh at themselves. I think if you can't laugh at yourself, you've got serious issues.

BO

There's one thing you must always do when you're on a night out, and that's wear deodorant. I call deodorant BOdorant. There is no need for anyone to have BO in this day and age. You can watch films on your phone and Skype people on the other side of the world, so there's no excuse for people to smell. It's not like we're living in Victorian times with tin baths. Soap and water are quite readily available.

When I was seventeen I worked with someone who had terrible BO and I had to have that awkward conversation with my manager about it. I didn't dare open my mouth when I was near that person in case I tasted it. Sometimes people smell like their clothes have been in a cupboard for weeks on end and I don't get that either. I don't understand why people can't smell themselves?

Some people really embrace their natural scent but I just couldn't. I'm sure even cave people rubbed flowers on their armpits. I'm sure they wouldn't have put up with that stench.

Whenever I'm on a train I can guarantee that someone near me will have BO and I get paranoid that it's me and I'm one of those people who can't smell themselves. I do that thing where I stretch and try to smell my armpits without anyone seeing. Or I'll spray deodorant straight onto my top while no one's looking, just in case. I'm dead cunning.

Manspreading

It does my head in when men spread their legs really wide when they're sat next to you on a train. It's inappropriate when they're touching your leg. That's my personal space. Piss off. There's a line on the seat and if they're over the crevice of the seat, they're in my area. I've asked men to move their legs before. It's just not appropriate.

If a man really spreads, you can see the shape of their balls and I don't want to be looking at that. It's not nice. Sometimes, if it's a big package, you can't help but look even though you really don't want to. It's like your eyes refuse to look anywhere else.

It's not just men who do it, I've see women do it too. It's worse when women have got a gunt and it's right in your face. Put it away.

Chat-up lines

I would say to any men who ever use chat-up lines, stop it. Unless someone is funny and charming when they're using them, they fall totally flat and they never work on me and my mates. If someone rolls out the 'Are you tired? Because you've been running through my mind all night' kind of lines and they're laughing while they're doing it, I don't mind that so much. But when someone genuinely tries to use a line and be cool with it? It's *awful*.

A guy once said to me, 'I've lost my phone, so can I have your number?' I was like, 'That makes *no* sense! How are you going to take my number if you've got no phone?' He clearly said the line completely wrong and as soon as he realized, he kind of scuttled off mambling.

The ten worst chat-up lines I've ever heard

1) Excuse me, my name's Mr Right, I was told you were looking for me?

2) Is that a ladder in your tights, or a stairway to heaven?

3) Does this rag smell like chloroform to you?

4) If I could rearrange the alphabet, I'd put U and I next to each other.

5) I bet your surname is Jacobs, cos you're a real cracker.

6) Have a feel of this shirt – do you know what that feels like? Boyfriend material.

7) You look like a parking ticket, because you've got 'fine' written all over you.

8) Are those astronaut trousers, cos your arse is out of this world.

9) Excuse me, do you have a plaster? I scraped my knee when I fell for you.

10) Can we shake hands? I want to be able to say I've been touched by an angel.

Wingwomen

Even though she's engaged, Sarah is my main wingwoman when we're out on the town because she's really friendly, and guys always seem to pick up on the fact that she's just being chatty and she's not interested in anything else. Which leaves room for me to move in . . .

She also knows a lot of guys through her fiancé, Michael, so that's a good way to meet lads. The best thing is that she knows me so well she can tell straight away if I'm not interested. All I need to do is raise my eyebrows a bit and she backs off. That's our code – it's the eyebrow code. I can't be wasting time on a lad I'm not keen on on a night out. There's dancing to be done.

I recently met a guy and when I woke up the following morning I had a text from him, but I *definitely* didn't give him my number. I think he got it from someone else somehow, so that worried me a bit. I've got my email address on my Twitter profile so that charities and stuff can contact me directly, and I've had lads sending me emails asking me out, which also makes me feel a bit uncomfortable. I haven't got my contact details on there so lads can crack on!

I've had messages on Facebook from guys saying they've seen me out the night before and asking me out for a drink. The first thing that goes through my head is, *Well, why didn't you come and speak to me then?* If a lad hasn't got the balls to come and talk to me in a bar, he's hardly the man of my dreams.

Having said that, I'm probably not that easy to approach. If I'm having proper banter with my mates and a lad comes up to me, I'm like, 'No, this is the wrong time. There are loads of girls sitting around waiting for lads to go up and talk to them and I'm in the middle of a dance-off. You need to get out of my personal space.'

I have tried to do a Cilla Black at times and introduce my mates to guys, but I'm so shit at it. I do it to Sam all the time and honestly, I'm crap. I've set her up with several of my male friends but matchmaking isn't my strong point. I still try, though. I want my friends to be happy and loved-up (but obviously not all of them before I am so I'm left on the shelf downing Blossom Hill on me own).

I don't know if anyone else does this, and if you don't it might seem a bit weird, but my mates and I sometimes take photos of lads we like on a night out. Not with their consent like, mainly when they're not looking. I like the way I moan about other people taking photos of me and then I do the same. But this is different. I could marry one of those men!

It does sound like we're a bunch of perverts, but we try and sneak pictures so we can show each other guys we fancy and get feedback. I did it in a restaurant recently and I didn't realize I had the flash turned on. This bloke looked at me as if to say, 'What the fuck?' and I had to say really loudly to my mate, 'This keeps happening with my phone, you know. It's dead weird.' I'm pretty sure I didn't get away with it.*

---

* I would just like to point out that taking photos of potential husbands is what I do when I'm not fussed about meeting a lad. Imagine what I'm like when I'm on it.

Music

As much as I love dancing on a night out, I'm not very up with the charts and shit. I couldn't tell you one song that's in the charts right now. I tend to dance to new stuff when I'm out but I never really know what's at number one. My iPhone playlist is one of those that you could *never* put on at a party. I'd be too embarrassed. I quite like sixties music, and I've even got a bit of B*Witched on my phone. I like old-school R&B too, and I've got a bit of early Kanye on there. I love his early stuff. But not that one where's he's on a motorbike with Kim. It made my ears bleed. And I can't work out if him saying he's Jesus and stuff is a joke or whether he really believes it.

My taste in music is basically shit.

Adele

I really like Adele. I just think everything she does is class. She doesn't have tits and arse in her videos. She's just about the songs. It's mental that she seems utterly unlike anyone else just because she's a normal size and shape. She's got shit from people on Twitter and again you just want to say to them, 'You're hearing those songs, the way she sings them, and what you're taking away from that is her weight?' It's just pathetic and I feel sorry for them. She's not even that big!

Funeral songs

I've also got my funeral songs on my iTunes. How weird is that? You know you're going to have one at some point, so you may as well sort it out now. My mam and I chat about our funeral songs *all* the time. We can't be the only ones? If we do it in front of Dad, he'll say, 'Will you not, please?' But we need to be organized because what if you hadn't chosen any song and someone played bad songs at your funeral? I wouldn't be able to rest. I'd be haunting everyone.

Mam's funeral songs are really emotional and she said she wants everyone to cry about how much they're going to miss her. She starts getting weepy when we talk about it, and she also gets upset about the fact she won't be at her own funeral.

When I walk into the church at my funeral – well, not walk in, when they take me in – I want 'Earth Angel' by the Penguins playing because it will get everyone crying. Then I want the 'Circle of Life' from *The Lion King*, and as they take me out I want 'My Way' by Frank Sinatra. You've got to be organized about this stuff.

I also want to arrive in a coach pulled by horses and I want people to wear black veils. I don't want anyone turning up in their work trousers because it's the only black thing they own; I want them to go out and buy special attire and big floppy hats. I don't want any of this 'It's a celebration' rubbish. I want loads of crying and people shouting, 'Why?!' I even know who I want the pallbearers to be. I've got a top-ten list because obviously I don't know who's still going to be around then, so I've got people as back-up. It's ridiculous that I haven't really planned my wedding but I know every detail of my funeral.

Top four songs that bring back memories

'Dancing Queen' by ABBA

This song instantly takes me back to the Winter Gardens in Blackpool. I'm transported back in time to dance competitions I took part in where I was covered in fake tan and glitter, choking on everyone's hairspray and hearing people cheering for each other. It's such a happy song.

'Wannabe' by the Spice Girls

This makes me think of my school-disco days when I had crimped hair, chunky trainers, roll-on glitter, flavoured lip gloss and blue eyeshadow. Stay classy, Scarlett.

'Jive Bunny Megamix'

This reminds me of my nanny's house at Christmas when I was a kid because it always got played. The children would be dancing around the living room while all the grown-ups frantically ran around trying to find chairs for everyone to sit on.

'I Gotta Feeling' by The Black Eyed Peas

Whenever I hear this I feel like I'm back at my old uni house getting ready for a night out. If Sarah didn't want to go out, I'd play this song and the next thing you knew it would be 5 a.m. and we'd be getting a Subway on the journey home.

Miley Cyrus

I love dancing to songs by Beyoncé on a night out, and I quite like Miley Cyrus too, but she's gone a bit crazy, hasn't she? It's not like she's leaking sex tapes and she never goes on about her weight or anything, she's just a bit quirky. She could do without mentioning drugs quite so much, but she's not offensive. Leave her be, I say.*

I think she's rebelling against Disney like Christina Aguilera and Britney Spears and Ariana Grande and Demi Lovato. I reckon there's a pattern there. They should take a look at what was going on in the Disney Club. Actually, that's a bit sick, isn't it, that so many of the sexy singers in the world are basically people we've grown up with as children. Mind you, my dad was around when Kylie was in *Neighbours* when she was dead young and now he thinks she's – how does he put it? – 'a very attractive woman'. He tried to get me to buy her calendar for him a little while ago and I wasn't having any of it.

Miley gets quite a lot of grief for not wearing much and making rude videos but I mean, she's not hurting anyone with the things she does. If you look back at Victorian times, it was slutty to show your ankles and we need to evolve eventually. No one has a problem with men having their tops off in music videos and they've been rapping about bitches and hos for ages. But when a woman says something controversial they all go mental.

I could never be a pop star. I was going to say it's because

---

* Although for any young people out there, that is not the correct way to operate a wrecking ball. She is not a good demolition role model.

I can't sing, but neither can most pop stars, can they? It's all about the auto-tune. Will.i.am sounds like a robot on his songs.

When it's raining or I'm sat in a car I pretend I'm in a music video. I'll put a ballad on and look out the window. I do it all the time. If no one is in the house, I'll pretend I'm auditioning for shows and things. I flick my hair back in the bath and belt out songs and all sorts. Everyone should do it. It's liberating.

The future of One Direction

I will admit to having danced to One Direction on a night out, but they've had it now, haven't they? I think they were on the wane before Zayn left to be honest, and then when he did a runner they kind of slipped even further in my estimation. Even though he'd left the band by the time he dumped Perrie the way he did, I think that whole thing tarnished them because he acted like such a twat. I also think they were for kids and then one of them got someone pregnant. That's when it was definitely time to call it a day.

1D needed to leave on a proper high so I think they split up at the right time. They needed to break up and then they can reunite in twenty years' time like all the other boy bands do. When they have a tax bill, or Marks & Spencer needs a new campaign.

Even my little sister thinks their music is crap. They look too old now and they haven't got that cute factor. They also seemed to get too big for their boots. I think Harry Styles is overrated. If anyone else had that hairstyle, they'd be called a knobhead. I quite like Niall because he keeps himself to himself and you never see him being an idiot in the papers. That's saying something about them: my favourite is the one I don't have to see as much.

Now they're going solo I think Harry Styles will be the only one that does well. Liam is probably the best singer but everyone fancies Harry. I can't imagine Louis being a big pop star. He'll just go and look after his kid. I'd like to think that Niall will come out of the woodwork and be a big solo star, but I can't see it.

I hope people realize what a dickhead Zayn is and that his music bombs. He thought he didn't need the band any more but time will tell. Seriously, who does he think he is? He's always having spats with celebrities like Calvin Harris and Naughty Boy. Who's looking after him? He's like this weird, angry little man. I don't think he'll do very well unless he stops being such a twat. I fear he'll start trying to rap. I'm genuinely scared about that.

I think it will be really hard for 1D not to have that fame any more, but maybe they'll enjoy being normal for a while? They can do little gigs in their local pubs and have a bit of craic.*

So, back to our night out. As long as I can actually see someone buy me a drink from a bar I'm fine with it. But anything

---

* To any One Direction fans who are on Twitter reading this, all that last bit was completely a joke. 1D are the best band in the world ever, obviously.

else? Forget it. A guy came up to me with a glass of wine recently and I told him I didn't want it. I was really nice about it but I was honest and said he could have put anything in it. He laughed, but I really meant it. People probably think I'm crazy but if in doubt, ask for the cash equivalent. Just think, if I took money every time someone offered to buy me a drink, I could end up *making* money on a night out!

Oddly I get bought fewer drinks now I'm on *Gogglebox*. I don't know if people think I'm rich or something? I'm sure people assume that as soon as you become even a bit famous you're absolutely loaded. I also wonder if people think I'm going to be dead up myself because I'm on telly so they don't approach me as much. But maybe it's just because they don't like my dance moves? What if I'm using *Gogglebox* as an excuse for being really offensive on the eyes and a shit dancer?

Ten things not to do on a night out (if you don't want to wake up with regret like I often do)

1) Go out without eating (always line your stomach).

2) Mix your drinks. This is where it all starts to go wrong. Stick to a maximum of two kinds of drink.

3) When it's your mate's round don't order something more expensive and be one of those people.

4) Ask the DJ to play a sad song or a ballad. You're on a night out, man. Keep things lively.

5) Spend half your night on your phone like a Wi-Fi wanker.

6) Think it's a good idea to text an ex.

7) Wear footwear you can't dance in. There's no point in having amazing shoes if they are going to be tucked under a table all night.

8) Try and take a selfie late at night. Take a tip from Cinderella and make midnight your cut-off point (I'm sure she took selfies).

9) Try and send a tweet or post on Facebook when you're very drunk. Or even slightly drunk.

10) Go home without getting food when you feel hungry. You'll only end up eating everything in your kitchen cupboards/fridge, and none of it will taste as nice as chips.

9
SCARLETT SAYS

. . . taxi!

Scarlett's Favourite Random Facts

Ostriches can run faster than horses.

Bananas are berries, strawberries are not.

When you die, your hair carries on growing for two months.

After countless drinks and a load of dancing it's time to head home. I tend to leave a night out once the room starts spinning, my feet begin to hurt or I've spent all of my money and used my credit card at least twice. Once my cash has gone and I've moved on to my card I know it's bad. You can get a double Jack Daniel's and Coke for £2.50 where I live, so I don't know how I spend so much money.

Sometimes I'll wake up the next morning and look at my online banking and my heart will drop. It's shocking. When I add that to how much cash I've taken out at the beginning of the night it's really depressing. I've basically paid a fortune to feel shit. I don't know why we all do it to ourselves?

I'm often up for extending a night when I'm out with the girls, so I've ended up at a lot of house parties whose sole purpose is to allow us to carry on drinking. Sometimes we don't even know the people whose house it is; we just roll up and drink some really shit wine.

I am one of those people who knows when to leave, though.

Knowing when to go home

It sounds crazy, but I have this weird sixth sense about when to go home. I get this funny feeling in my stomach and I know shit's going to go down, so I toddle off. I usually pretend I'm going to the loo and then try and leave. I never tell my friends I'm off because I know they'd try and make me stay; I just do a sly slip-away.

One of my mates will usually phone me the following day and say, 'You left at the right time. There was a big fight and things got smashed.' I feel really smug knowing I was at home asleep when all of that was going on.

There is a bit of etiquette for leaving places and I think it says a lot about a person how they do it. Some of my friends get dead stressed about it and they'll make sure they go round and say goodbye to every single person before they go, but I can't be arsed. Sometimes I'll admit I'm leaving, but most of the time I'll disappear and then send a message to our Facebook group to say I'm in a taxi and not to worry about me.

One of my friends never knows when it's time go to bed. We literally have to tell her she needs to leave when she's swaying and singing. You never want to be that person who wakes up on someone else's sofa with a mouth drier than the Sahara, but that's always her.

Another friend is like the face of British binge drinking. I'll always have to take her for some food to try and sober her up after a night out. She'll be eating with her hands, and her face and clothes will be covered in food. I do look at her sometimes and think, *How are you the one that's engaged? How does someone love you so much it's OK to eat like that?*

She always wants to go on to Monaco's and carry on the night after she's eaten, but then once we get in she leaves after about five minutes. Sam, Kelly and I are usually the hardcore ones.

Kelly is generally the last person to go home because she'll bump into someone she knows and attach herself to them. Even if she's not really good friends with that person she'll stay out so she can carry on partying.

Drunken collecting

I don't know why but I seem to collect random things on a night out. I once got home with only one shoe and a 'party upstairs' sign. I've also woken up with a lot of toilet signs in my bag. I know it's theft but when I'm drunk it's just so funny. I don't know why I do it. I must just peel them off doors. The worst thing I woke up with was one of those massive yellow 'wet floor' signs. I left it in the living room by mistake and my parents were horrified. Christ, I'm going to get banned from all the clubs in my area. We've got drawers full of them little Argos pencils at home. We've even got pens from when they had pens, so it must run in the family.

Taxi bribery

Getting home from my own home town is really easy because I only live a five-minute walk away. I'll still get a taxi, though. Me dad wouldn't be happy if I walked home. One thing I do that's really bad is pay the taxi driver in food. I reckon that happens about four times out of ten. Right near the taxi rank there's a place called Pizza Zone and I'll get a slice of pizza, some chips and a tub of garlic sauce, which is £2.50. But you don't get many chips so I'll often get another tub.

As soon as I get into Pizza Zone my shoes will come off, and then I get the shock of looking in their mirrors. They've got really unflattering strip lighting and giant mirrors so I look terrible. My lipstick will be halfway up my face and my eyelashes will be hanging off and winking at people. Amazingly Sam always pulls in there – I don't know why because no one looks good in that lighting.

When I get in the cab I've usually only got about 50p left in my purse, so say the taxi is a fiver, I'll offer the driver my chips instead. Half the time they're starving so they'll just take them, but sometimes they're arseholes and they'll drive me to a cashpoint near Asda to get some actual cash.

The first thing I do when I get out of the taxi is scramble about for my key, and then drop it as soon as I find it. Then I have to turn on the torch on my phone to find the keyhole. I find myself telling the door to be quiet because it sounds so loud when I'm trying to get it to actually fit. I swear the keyhole shrinks or becomes a totally different shape when I'm drunk because I can open it perfectly fine when I'm sober. It's like trying to fit a giraffe into a bungalow.

If I haven't already taken my shoes off in the taxi, they come off as soon as I get through the door so I don't make too much noise. Even if I've had a load of food from Pizza Zone I'll still eat more random food. I'll eat whatever's in the house, like Camembert and shit. Who the fuck comes back from a night out and eats a whole baked Camembert? Me, it seems.

I'll also make myself peanut butter sandwiches or drunk toast with *everything* on it.

Sometimes when I wake up the day after a night out and go into the kitchen I'll feel dead proud because I've managed not to go and get food on the way home. Then me mam will say, 'Yeah, you did. There was an empty pizza box and some rogue chips on the floor.' In my mind, if I don't remember it, it didn't happen.

The make-up dilemma

I always promise myself I'm going to take all my make-up off, drink loads of water and take paracetamol when I get home, but when you're drunk that seems like a lot of hard work. So quite often I won't even take my make-up off, and I wake up looking like Freddie Krueger. Don't most women do that, though?

I don't know if it's a contouring thing or what, but quite often all of the make-up from the middle of my face will have wiped off and all the make-up at the side of my face is still there looking very dark. I'll have loads of foundation around my hairline and a glowing white patch in the middle.

When I eventually wipe my make-up off I'll have a really brown body and a really white face because I don't bother to fake-tan my face. I just use a ton of bronzer instead. As a result I look like I've got a floating head. It looks like it belongs to someone else. And that's pretty much how I feel after a big night out.

I try my hardest not to wake anyone up when I'm making drunk food, but me dad always seems to know when I'm back and he'll appear at the top of the stairs asking me if I'm all right, which always makes me feel a lot drunker than I am. There's me thinking I'm being dead quiet like a cat burglar and yet he still hears me.

A lot of the time I won't actually make it up to my bed because the sofa always looks dead comfy and I can't be bothered to walk up the stairs. Even if it's minus ten downstairs I'll convince myself I'll be fine, but then I'll wake up shivering, covered in the smallest blanket imaginable.

Right before I go to sleep I'll start looking at Sam's Snapchat. She posts so often I feel like I'm still bloody out! I swear she thinks she's doing a BBC documentary on one of our nights out. She'll Snapchat one of us having a drink and I'm like, 'No one gives a shit.' She'll also post videos saying, 'We're going to the champagne bar now,' and I'm like, 'You've got about twenty people on your Snapchat and half of those people are here. Who are you doing this for?'

As soon as I close my eyes and get comfortable it feels like I'm on a waltzer. The whole room starts spinning and for some reason I think if I close my eyes more tightly it will make it better, but in actual fact it just makes it worse. It's horrible.

I do really weird things before I go to bed too. I once woke up and I couldn't move my hands and I couldn't work out what was wrong. I was really worried, and then I realized I'd put socks on them. I vaguely remember thinking I didn't want my fake tan to rub off, so that must have been why I did it.

10
SCARLETT SAYS

...*me head hurts*

Scarlett's Favourite Random Facts

Scotland's national animal is the
unicorn.

You're twice as likely to be
killed by a vending machine as
you are to be bitten by a shark.

Human thigh bones are stronger than
concrete.

My hangover will generally last until Sunday evening when I find myself sitting around thinking, *What is my life? Where's it going?* For some reason I also think about the past. I mull over things I've done and places I've been, and I wonder how my life would be if I'd made different decisions. It feels a bit like those *Dungeons and Dragons* books where you can change the entire outcome of the book depending on which page you turn to next.

If I'm feeling really sorry for myself, I'll spend the early part of the evening downstairs with my parents and my little sister drinking loads of tea and eating more food.

I like hanging out with my mam and dad when I'm hungover because it's comforting. That may sound weird but if you get it, you'll get it, and if you don't, you'll just think I'm odd. We all like watching the same programmes, so there are never any arguments over what's on telly.

Even if I've had loads of sleep – which is rare – I still feel like I've only slept for about half an hour if I've been drinking. At about 7 a.m. my entire family will come downstairs and start banging around (OK, making a cup of tea, but it feels bloody loud) and I'll be like, 'Why are you doing this to me? I only got in two hours ago.'

Me mam never lets me sleep in when I'm hungover. It's

like my punishment for getting drunk. She always says that I'm wasting the day, but even if I'm up I'm going to waste the day because I'm not a fully functioning person. I'm much better off lying in bed. I've had days when I've moved back to my bedroom from the sofa and tried to sleep all day but I still felt bloody awful in the evening. It's so annoying when you can't sleep when you're hungover because you know it's the one thing that will help you. It's all that Red Bull in the Jäger-bombs.

There's nothing worse than waking up and literally not knowing what's going on. I've had hangovers where I feel like I'm having an out-of-body experience and I start questioning everything. The worst thing I can do is lie in bed thinking, *I'm wasting my life*. That happens a lot when I've mixed my drinks. For some reason that makes it worse.

I don't mind the hangovers where you feel like you're still drunk because they can be quite funny, but I hate those ones where you feel like you're all right and then it creeps up on you. You order loads of food and you can't eat it, and all of a sudden at 2 p.m. your head starts playing tricks on you and you begin to overanalyse everything. You worry that you've done awful things and you need to change your life. I can see why people traditionally went to church on a Sunday – you need a bit of comfort, like. But I'd feel wrong if I went there, cos I can't be in a place of God when I'm hungover, can I? With the vodka sweats and that. You don't want to be saying the Lord's name when you've still got the shakes from Red Bull.

What's in my bedside cabinet?

Fake tan and a fake-tan mitt (I always keep my tanning tools to hand)

A *Hunger Games* book

A packet of Parma Violets

A lighter for my candle for when I want a bit of ambience while I watch *EastEnders*

Some circular batteries (no idea where they came from)

Five pens, of which only one works

Hangover food

If the girls and I go out on a Saturday night, we'll always go for Sunday dinner the following day. I'll lie in bed and wait for someone to write a message to our Facebook group saying, 'Who's going for food?' Quite often we'll either go to The March Hare, which does two-for-one Sunday dinners. We'll get two each and sit there with a topknot and no make-up on, not talking at all. Food gets me through a hangover.

Sometimes if I'm really hungover and I know that Ivo, who is my best boy friend, has been out too I'll message him and arrange to meet at McDonald's for breakfast. Sundays are the only day you're allowed to eat yourself into a coma without feeling guilty.

When I was at uni I never used to get hangovers. We would always stay out until 6 a.m. because that was when the McDonald's breakfasts started. I'd have one of them, go home, have some sleep, get up and go to a lecture, and even go to work. I barely even knew I'd been out. They definitely get worse as you get older. Not that it seems to be stopping me, like.

Whenever I'm hungover I just want to eat beige food, and when I had a terrible hangover recently I ordered myself a 'Couples Treat' deal from Domino's, even though it was only me eating it. When I told me dad I was going to get pizza he offered to cook me some prawns. Why? Has anyone with a shit hangover ever said, 'Do you know what I really fancy? Some prawns.' They weren't even battered ones because at least deep-fried food is comforting. They were just plain old pink things.

The problem is, me dad is quite health conscious but I'm not, so he tries to make me feel guilty for ordering bad food. I'll be eating mozzarella dippers and I'll notice he's on his phone but he keeps looking over at me. Suddenly he'll say, 'You know there are 1,200 calories in those?' But I just don't care. Every time someone tells you the calorie content of something it ruins it slightly, and I just want to eat my pizza in peace.

I absolutely have to have garlic sauce with pizza. Garlic sauce says a lot about where you are in the country. Up north it's proper mayo, but the further down south you go the waterier it gets and it's really disappointing. I'm genuinely thinking about starting to carry my own around with me when I travel.

I have gone through phases of eating too much pizza. When I was at uni they used to know our order when we phoned up, and last year my family and I got a Christmas

card from our local pizza takeaway, which is never a good sign. Melted cheese is amazing on pizzas. In fact, on anything. All cheese is good, apart from cheese in a can. That is the most wrong thing I've ever heard of.

Fast food

Fast food is self-explanatory. I hate waiting for ages in restaurants if I'm hungry and by the time the meal's arrived I've eaten so much of the bread they give you while you're waiting I'm full up. If you go to a fast food restaurant, your order is there in seconds and you're like, 'Wham, bam, thank you, ma'am.' I know it's all processed and there's about 5 per cent meat in the burger but do I care? No. It tastes bloody lovely. I'm the same with kebab meat. I know it's a bit mysterious, but so what? I like a bit of mystery. What's life without risk?

I'm more of a Burger King than McDonald's girl because their burgers are proper and they do bigger chips, but I do wish someone would deliver McDonald's breakfasts to my bed when I'm hungover.

Morgan Spurlock did that film, *Super Size Me*, where he ate McDonald's every day for a month and got really ill, and it gave fast food a really bad name. But who the fuck would eat a McDonald's every day? Seriously? If you ate carrots for every meal for a month, you'd probably turn a weird colour. Why doesn't he try that instead of making us feel bad for eating plastic cheese? Everything in moderation.

Greggs

There's a twenty-four-hour Greggs in Newcastle airport. I wrote about it on Twitter the other day and Greggs messaged me to ask if I wanted a festive box. All I could imagine was like fifty sausage rolls in a box that you'd have to eat really quickly before they got cold. There are certain sorts of food that you have to have hot.

Ten foods you didn't know existed

1) Canned whole chicken

2) Squirty cheese (I thought plastic slices were gross enough)

3) Tuna eyeballs (No words)

4) Marshmallow fluff

5) Pork brains in milk gravy (DAFUQ?)

6) Fermented eggs

7) Squeezy bacon (Yes. Squeezy. Bacon)

8) Bacon jam (it exists)

9) Canned fish mouths

10) Cheeseburger in a tin (that's McNasty)

Coffee shops

I've never really got the whole coffee-shop crap. Everything about them confuses me. I don't understand why people always meet in them? All they sell is sandwiches and bad coffee. And I would never go anywhere where people serve you drinks in a polystyrene cup. They're dirty, they are.

I feel awkward when I go into a coffee shop. The seats are always dead low so you slide off them, and they write your name on your cup. That's stalkerish.

Ordering is also really confusing. A medium coffee is called a tall, and a large one is a venti. What the fuck does 'venti' mean? Why not just call them small, medium and large? Poor old people when they go in there. They must not have a clue what to ask for. It's a coffee minefield.

My home town is really tiny and even we've got a Costa Coffee and a Starbucks. I don't understand why they're so expensive. They must be making a bomb. I've got a tip for you: if you've got £4, rather than spend it on one coffee in a coffee chain, go to Asda and buy yourself some coffee and some milk, and that will last you a good few days.

My friend Bam told me once she'd got a job as a barista, and I thought she meant like a legal barrister, so I was well impressed. I was buzzing for her and said we needed to go out and celebrate. Then I found out she was going to work in Caffè Nero and it wasn't quite as exciting.

Eating out

My mates and I really like eating out and we go to Nando's all the time, because that's a given. It is basically overpriced chicken, but it's *nice* overpriced chicken. I also like a pub dinner. We used to go to steak night at Wetherspoons religiously for a catch-up, but we don't seem to do that much any more.

If the girls and I are feeling fancy, we'll go to Fat Buddha in Durham for dinner because that does really nice cocktails, but normally we'll go to Mama Bella or Spice Island in Bishop Auckland.

One time we went out for Sam's birthday and we had our own private room upstairs. We organized a cake with loads of sparklers on and it set the sprinklers off. We were crying with laughter and we had to open the windows to try and stop the water spraying out, but the staff didn't even bother to come upstairs. When we went downstairs and told them they just shrugged and said, 'Yeah, it's not a lot of water, though, is it?' We were soaked and the cake was ruined, but it kind of made the night.

We used to go to this Italian restaurant near where I lived. If it was your birthday, they'd make you drink those shitty limoncello shots and get you to stand on the table while they danced around you.

Me mam and I always go to a place called The Goodie Box, which does amazing hot chocolate. It's a cafe but it also sells candles and balloons for any occasion. You can get two main meals and drinks in there for about £7. If you go in there with a tenner, you can get three courses and a bottle of wine. Seriously, it's crazily cheap.

Something that does my head in is kids in pubs. If you can't keep your kids under control, don't bring them out to eat. Don't ruin it for the rest of us who don't have kids, or have left them at home. I shouldn't have to put up with kids shouting when I'm eating my lunch. I've had to leave places before because six- and seven-year-olds are running around our table being really annoying. There should be a separate area for kids in the same way they used to have smoking and non-smoking areas.

Another thing that annoys me is people snogging each other over the table when they're out for dinner. It's minging. Sometimes people will take a mouthful of their food and kiss each other and I'm like, 'What are you doing?' If a couple were in a pub together, they wouldn't start kissing across the table and being all lovey-dovey, but for some reason they think it's OK to do it in a restaurant. It's *really* not. I don't even like it when a lad holds me hand at the table. We're not in a movie and you're not Colin Firth. We can just eat and have a chat, you know.

Cooking

My signature dish is crackers, beans and cheese, which is what I always ate when I was a student. It's like a cheap version of beans on toast. You get a cracker, a tablespoon of beans and put some cheese on top and microwave it.

Cooking to me is when you use pans and shit, and I can cook soup and stuff in them, but that's all I can do. Me dad bought a dozen eggs recently so he could teach me how to make a soft-boiled egg and it took me eight attempts to get it right, even though I was using a timer. I don't understand it.

People come into work with homemade lasagne and I don't get that. Why not just go and buy one? Look at how complicated Jamie Oliver's recipes are. Who has all that shit in their cupboards? Who has those spices? When I watch *The Great British Bake Off* and they're making their own pastry I don't understand why. Why not just go and buy some of the ready-made stuff? I'm basically mint at ordering food, but I'm not great in the kitchen.

Call centres

It stresses me out when I have to phone call centres myself. The other day our internet stopped working, which meant no Netflix. I started having a proper panic and it turned out that when me dad changed banks the direct debit didn't get transferred over so they'd cut it off. He phoned to pay the bill and they started asking what his dog's name was and what his email address from eight years ago was, and they were being really difficult. He was like, 'I just want to pay. I'm giving *you* money!' In the end he said he was going to change internet providers and all of a sudden they made it really easy for him. Why go through all of that?

I have to get me mam or dad to phone call centres for me because I lose my temper. Sometimes it's dead muffled and I can't understand what they say and it's so frustrating. Or when you phone and try and book tickets for something and it's automated and you have to give your name, I'll say, 'Scarlett Moffatt,' as clearly as possible and it'll come back and say, 'Carol Henderson. Is this correct?' Nooooo! It's bloody not! I would happily pay a company to deal with call centres on my behalf. Someone's missing a trick with that. Maybe I should go on *Dragon's Den*?

My five favourite foods

1) Beans on toast
Yes, it's simple and, yes, it's probably one of the main reasons the French think we have zero culinary skills, but there's nothing better than getting home, putting the TV on, making a nice cup of tea and having the dinner of champions.

2) Sunday dinner
This is not to be confused with Christmas dinner because that involves different meat and also has the added bonus of pigs in blankets. A proper Sunday roast instantly takes me back to my nanny's house and the sound of people arguing about how much a Fabergé egg is worth on *Antiques Roadshow*.

3) Chicken fajitas
This is mainly because it's the only thing I can make that doesn't come in a tin. I also like food where you don't have to use a knife and fork, and I have a slight addiction to jalapeños.

4) Pizza
I'm not even that fussy about what toppings I have, as long as it's not pineapple. No one wants one of their five a day on their pizza.

5) Chocolate
Dark, milk, white . . . Any kind of chocolate instantly puts me in a good mood.

My perfect TV night in

One of the reasons I love being a part of *Gogglebox* is because I'm such a fan of TV. If I was staying in on my own for my perfect evening, I would watch *EastEnders* and at least one episode of *RuPaul's Drag Race*. As I've mentioned before, I also like *Red Dwarf*, *Bottom* and *The Young Ones*. I'm always trying to get my friends into those shows but they're not having it. I know the words to all of the episodes.

If I'm with all the girls, we'll have to watch *Keeping Up With the Kardashians*, which I hate. They're properly into it, but I think it's shit. We tend to watch a film too. *Magic Mike* is a good one, and also *Dirty Dancing*, *The Notebook* and *Ghost* are ones we watch over and over again. Stuff we can cry to, basically.

Five films I love

La Vita è Bella (Life is Beautiful)
It's the only subtitled film that I love. It's so amazing you forget about them. It's about a dad who pretends a concentration camp is a game so his son doesn't get scared. It's so sad but so beautiful.

Edward Scissorhands
The fact I still find Johnny Depp attractive when he's got scissors for hands, a penchant for PVC and scars all over his face probably makes me a bit odd, but I want a boyfriend like Eddy. You'd always have a decent haircut with him around.

Beauty and the Beast

I feel like it teaches us the dangers of going out with a 'roid-head like Gaston. But the scene when he gives Belle the library is one of my favourite ever. Plus you can sing along.

Pitch Perfect

This is amazing. Fat Amy, nerds singing and a riff off. What more do you need in a film?

Bridesmaids

This film changed chick flicks. It reminds me so much of my friendship group it's scary, but I'm definitely not the one who shits herself in the street.

Downton Abbey

One show I cannot stand is *Downton Abbey*, and we're *so* happy as a family that it's ending. We hate it. Me mam's bought some champagne to celebrate the end of it.

Nothing ever happens in it! It's so boring. Surely back then everyone would have been getting frisky? It's so crap.

I know I'm probably alone in this but I think people only like *Downton* because everyone else does. They just jumped on the bloody bandwagon. It's a bit like when Adele did her big comeback with 'Hello'. You daren't say you don't like the song in case people have a go at you, but it wasn't that great. I also think Sam Smith is really overrated. I think he's *all right*, but he's not the world's greatest singer ever, is he?

The Great British Bake Off

Oh my God, I love *TGBBO*. Pies and tarts week is my favourite. Mary Berry is like my adopted grandmother – I just love her. The hosts' innuendos are brilliant and I'm always tweeting about them. I like their 'deep cracks' and 'big buns'. I also think it's great because it's encouraging people to bake (I'm not one of those people, mind).

It's Ava's favourite programme and she'll shout, 'It's meringue week,' and get really excited, and I'm like, 'Calm your boots.'

Sometimes some of the baking looks like dog shit on a plate and the judges will eat it and say, 'Eee, that's delicious,' which really makes me laugh.

Some of the things the contestants make are incredible. When that man made a lion out of bread it was genius. A lion! Out of bread! They're like Gordon Ramsay crossed with Van Gogh.

Talent shows

There seem to be more and more talent shows every time I switch on my telly, but I do like them. Well, most of them.

I used to like *The X Factor* when it was just four judges in a room with no music and no audience for the auditions. That's when it was funny. Now it's all about what people are wearing and it's all really posh. What happened to it being simple? I miss Louis too. He balanced out the judges and stopped Simon looking dead old compared to the others.

Simon has turned into a bit of a sap since he's become a

parent. He did get tougher later on in the last series but early on it felt like he was censoring himself. I liked it when he was really honest with people and told them they'd never make it in showbiz. I mean, I know he was shattering dreams, but at least he was being kind not wasting their time.[*]

I do watch some people and think, *Why are your mam and dad not telling you you're shit? Don't they like you enough?* My parents would definitely tell me I can't sing for toffee, and I'd much rather they did. Although having said that, I tried karaoke for the first time the other night. I did 'Let it Go' from *Frozen* and I felt like I nailed it, but I'm pretty sure if you asked the other people in the room they wouldn't agree. Some people just need to realize that there's some things that are indoor things and not for public consumption.

The X Factor does shit all over *The Voice*, though. Where do the winners of *The Voice* go? You literally never hear from them again. It's like they've been kidnapped. Maybe Tom Jones has got them locked up in his basement for entertainment?

The best thing about *The Voice* is the swivelly chairs, but they need more crap contestants. Everyone on there is too good. I think you need a mixture on a talent show. You need to have some funny, awful people to provide some humour.

I do love *Britain's Got Talent* too. I think it's a really good representation of what the UK is about – eccentricity. If someone came to Britain from another country and you wanted to show them what we're all about, you could show them an

_____

[*] I don't know what that says about me, like.

episode of *BGT* and they'd get it. It's full of the odd bods and shows you everything that's good about the UK. Who doesn't want to see someone playing a flute with their nose? Yes, it's shit, but it's funny.

I refuse to watch shows like *Flockstars*. I watched about ten minutes of one episode and I couldn't understand what it was all about. I thought it might have been a joke but it really was about people herding sheep. That, in my opinion, was a step too far.

Eternal Glory

The one I really can't believe is the one with all the former athletes. They have rounds like standing on one leg. It's just ridiculous. I watched it the other day – I'm not kidding, the first round was a staring competition, the next round tiddly-winks. And the third round was a very intense game of hopscotch. I'd be more impressed if they were all standing up somewhere for a nine-hour shift.

Drunk posts

I like to watch as much TV as possible on a hangover Sunday, but for some reason, usually when I'm watching *Antiques Roadshow*, I'll start remembering all the things I did the night before and it's *awful*. I'll think about the people I texted or the photos I posted. I have to check my Snapchat, Twitter, Insta-gram and Facebook in case there's anything I can't remember, and I delete anything I need to. It's weird because sometimes I don't worry about it, but every now and again I'll get one of those hideous panicky hangovers and I feel like I need to do some proper deep-breathing exercises.

You should never drink and post, generally. It never works out well, does it? It's almost as bad as drunk dialling an ex. In fact, why doesn't everyone just leave their phones at home on a night out? Ah yes, that's right, because they're like our third hand and we'd have a meltdown.

Hangover cures

I think hangovers are God's punishment because he believes binge drinking is a sin. While you're drinking you're loving life, but then you have the fallout. I just don't really understand why it was OK for Jesus to encourage binge drinking but it's not OK for us to do it?

How the hell has no one come up with a hangover cure that works yet? Or a drink that doesn't make you feel like someone is drilling inside your head the following day? I don't understand how we can send people to the moon but no one can make you feel less shit after a night out.

The only thing that sometimes makes me feel better the following day is a big pack of Haribo and some orange Lucozade. A couple of my friends will have wheatgrass shots but that would make me vomit. I have tried it but it literally tastes like you're eating grass, and I'm not a fucking cow, like.

Hangry

I think this is a really important new word. Sometimes you're furious at someone and you don't really know why and then you realize it's because you need to eat and that explains it, I reckon.

Abstinence

Of course, when I feel really bad I swear I'm going to stop drinking for a while. I did stop for a month once when I did Dry January in aid of Cancer Research. It was for a good cause so that side of it was great, but it was proper torture. It's tradition that on New Year's Day me and all the girls go on a pub crawl in our home town. Everyone was so drunk and I was drinking water. I knew if I started drinking Coke I'd want to put a vodka in it, and I ended up having to go home early.

I felt really ill for the first couple of weeks, so I went to the doctor and she said it was because my body was used to drinking. How bad is that? All the toxins were leaving my body like a mini detox. But by the end of the month I had more energy and I'd lost weight, even though I was eating more, so it did make me think I should carry on. But then I thought, *Nah*.

Come 1 February I had my first drink for thirty-one days and I got drunk off about two Jack Daniel's and Cokes. At least I know I can give up for a month again if I want to. Which I don't.

My top ten hangover foods

1) Orange Lucozade

2) Scotch eggs with Nutella (sounds awful but it's amazing)

3) Crackers, beans and melted cheese

4) A dunk, aka a cup of tea and biscuits. Preferably hobnobs because they're sturdy

5) Chips and garlic sauce

6) McDonald's breakfast sausage and egg McMuffin

7) Leftover pizza

8) Any takeaway containing carbs

9) Bacon sandwich with lots of tomato sauce

10) Black Pudding

Moving out

My mam and dad make jokes about the fact I'll still be living with them when I'm sixty, but I know they don't really want me to go. I do want to move out, but what will I do when I've got a shit hangover? I'll have to go home and get looked after.

Mam keeps trying to convince me that getting my own place is a bad idea and saying, 'Think of what you could buy with the money you'll be spending on rent.' She even worked out how much I would be paying for all my bills and she con-

---

* Tequila for breakfast is never a good option, despite what your friends say. A slice of lemon is not one of your five a day.

verted it into how many pairs of shoes I could buy each month. She literally said to me, 'If you keep this money in a pot, by the end of the month you could buy *all* of these things. You could even go on holiday!' It did make me see things differently, to be fair.

My dad always says that I don't have to pay board and he also comes up with reasons I should stay but I will have to go eventually. Hopefully within the next couple of years I'll do it. I may have to pack one day while my parents are doing the food shopping and leave them a change of address card and a housewarming invitation.

I think they would miss me and I would miss them loads too. Although I lived by myself at uni for three years and I really liked it, even though our place was an absolute shithole. It was hard work at times, having to do our own cleaning and shit, but I liked it.

I think when you reach your mid-twenties you start to feel like you should be more independent. You see everyone on Facebook posting photos of keys, saying, 'Moving into my new place,' and you think, *Maybe that should be me*. Even when I do move out I'll still take my washing back home. I'm not buying a bloody washing machine. I'm not made of money.

Roman re-enactments

We do some really random shit as a family. There's a place called Binchester Roman Fort near us and they do Roman re-enactments. I won't lie, my family and I have been known to go along and join in. It sounds proper sad, but I have dressed up as a Roman soldier before.

Sometimes we go metal detecting around there as well, although you have to give back everything you find. My dad properly loves it and it can be fun. Some people once got a Roman mannequin and put an 'I Heart Ibiza' top, some leg-warmers and a visor on it. It was mint.

Yes, you do look a bit like a wanker, and I'm not going to meet the man of my dreams down at the fort because most of them are old with long, dirty fingernails and they remind me of the blokes off *Time Team*.

I felt brave once so I posted a picture of meself with a severed head wearing a full suit of armour on Facebook. My friends were like, 'This is why you're single.' But if a lad can't see past a severed head and a metal outfit, he's not the one for me anyway.

I don't often tell my friends when I do it. If they ask where I've been, I'll say I've been for lunch with my mam and dad and Ava. I don't want it to be like, 'What did you do today?' 'Oh, I took part in a Roman re-enactment.'

Christmas

Christmas is all about family and I love it. What is there not to like about it? If you don't like it, I think there's something properly wrong with you.

Me mam is a Grinch. She loves buying presents but she hates decorations. We once had a black Christmas tree – a *black* Christmas tree – because we had a new black leather couch and she wanted it to match. It was pissing awful.

Me dad is the total opposite and he would have the whole house covered in tackiness if he could. We stick crap up everywhere and it drives me mam mad because all the baubles have to match. She has a festive battle on her hands.

Ava loves Christmas too and I want to take her to Lapland one day, but I'm so sad she's cottoned on to the fact Santa's not real. (Sorry if I've ruined that for you.) She said to me recently, 'Santa is just your mam and dad,' and I was nearly crying, going, 'No, it *isn't!*' I'm gutted.

At Christmas there are usually about sixteen of us around the dinner table. My nanny and granddad's house is tiny so we're all sat on different-sized chairs and by the time the roast potatoes make it to the other end of the table they're stone cold, but no one gives a shit.

We always play bingo at Christmas, and we have quizzes. My nanny always does the quiz and every year it's about *Carry On* films. I'm sure she uses the same one year after year. She always joins a team even though we moan about how unfair it is. Funnily enough, her team always wins. It would be a real worry if they didn't.

Jesus

My family and I had a long discussion about Jesus the other day. It was a bit heavy for a Friday afternoon like, but it was interesting. After all, this is the man who gave us the gift of Christmas.

So it turns out me mam thinks Jesus was just like an old-fashioned Dynamo and my dad thinks he was a doctor, which is why he healed loads of lepers and shit.

Personally I think Jesus was probably a bit like Derren Brown and he could do amazing tricks so everyone thought he was the man. Maybe in another 2,000 years there will be an amazing new celebration in Derren's name. Although Derrenmas doesn't really work, does it?

Pets

When my Sunday night hangover all gets too much I have to go upstairs and find a way to distract myself. I'll go to bed and read loads of shit online or watch YouTube videos of *X Factor* fails until I fall asleep. Sometimes Ava will come and watch things with me, and my dog Bonnie will be there having a cuddle.

I love pets. They're such a big part of your family. I got a snake called Cecil for my tenth birthday, but when I went on holiday when I was thirteen I left him with my mam's friend Dawn and he 'escaped'.

My theory is that my mam asked Dawn to give him away because she hated him. We used to have a patterned carpet and he would regularly escape from his tank and blend in with the carpet. She would always freak out when she spotted him slithering around, so I reckon she hatched a plan to get rid of poor Cecil.

I also had a frog called Stony and a fish I won from the fair called Lucky. That's the one my dad cut the thumb off a glove for; he put Lucky inside and then we gave him a proper burial. We did the same with all me hamsters. We had one called Gladiator because he used to climb on top of the cage and he was mint, but they don't last long, do they?

We love dogs as a family and we had a Labrador called Glenn when I was younger, and now we've got Harry and

Bonnie. We like quite human names for our pets. Harry is named after Prince Harry, and Bonnie is called Miss Bonnie Blue Butler after Scarlett O'Hara's daughter in *Gone with the Wind*. Chihuahuas are Mexican and for Halloween last year I got Bonnie a little sombrero and some legwarmers that had maracas attached to them. She looked amazing.

I would never want a cat. I hate them. They don't give a fuck and they're selfish. If someone else starts feeding them, they'll instantly be their best friend, even if you've had them for years.

Charlotte, who I sit next to at work, had a cat for about seven years and the people in the house opposite her kept feeding it. She asked them to stop but they didn't and now the cat lives with her neighbours and refuses to go home. It sits in the window looking at Charlotte with a smug look on its face.

Cats are like blokes: they piss off and come back whenever they want feeding.

Dreams

After I've watched loads of random crap on YouTube, my light will go out at about nine o'clock because by that point I've had enough of my hangover. That's all I can take. I know I'll wake up feeling better on the Monday so I want it to come as quickly as possible.

I often remember my dreams and I have dead weird ones. Whenever one of my friends has a weird dream they'll message me and ask me what it means. I've got this app on my phone with the meanings of things, so I'll analyse it for them.

I used to have this recurring dream that I was being

chased by a fox and I'd go up in my attic to hide, but it would already be up there. It could never quite catch me, though. Apparently that means I'm worrying about things I shouldn't be worrying about.

I hate it if I wake up and don't remember my dreams because I like being able to tell people about them. I had a dream about Jason Manford once and I woke up and sort of fancied him afterwards, which was weird. I also had one about my ex cheating on me and I was really pissed off with him the next day because it felt so real.

I once dreamt I got a work promotion, and I also dreamt that I was a kids' TV presenter. I'm really hoping that one comes true.

So, we've come to the end of our night out/hangover day. I hope you've had fun. I have to say, the worst thing after a big weekend is going to work on a Monday still feeling hungover because it's always busy and everyone is asking me loads of questions. That's when I'll tell myself I'm never drinking again. But then by the Tuesday when I feel OK, I'm back to loving life, all those plans I made on Sunday to be really healthy go out the window and I'm gearing up for a weekend of binge drinking again. And hell, Saturday is only five days away . . .

Scarlett xx

Acknowledgements

I'd like to thank so many people for the opportunity to write my own book! First of all, the gang at Studio Lambert: Stephen Lambert, the CEO; Tania Alexander, the director of Factual Entertainment and Queen of *Gogglebox*; Harriet Manby, the *Gogglebox* cast manager for keeping everything running smoothly; Gemma Scholes, the production manager, and all the lovely crew who make the whole thing so much fun. Huge thanks to all at Channel 4 who, every year, find new ways to do even more with the show, especially David Glover.

I'd also like to thank all at LAW, especialy Julian Alexander for their work on making the book a reality. Thank you to Jordan Paramor for being such a great co-pilot.

Thanks to the gang at Pan Macmillan for being such a good publisher; Jamie Coleman was always there with pizza, drinks and suggestions for famous people I could be annoyed at.

Special thanks to my family and friends; I'm so lucky to have you and I'm grateful every day.

extracts reading groups
competitions books new
discounts extracts
competitions
books new
events books
extracts interviews
discounts
events
www.panmacmillan.com
extracts events reading groups
competitions books extracts new